Enforcing the Convict Code

Enforcing the Convict Code

Violence and

Prison Culture

Rebecca Trammell

LYNNE
RIENNER
PUBLISHERS

BOULDER
LONDON

Published in the United States of America in 2012 by
Lynne Rienner Publishers, Inc.
1800 30th Street, Boulder, Colorado 80301
www.rienner.com

and in the United Kingdom by
Lynne Rienner Publishers, Inc.
3 Henrietta Street, Covent Garden, London WC2E 8LU

Library of Congress Cataloging-in-Publication Data
Trammell, Rebecca.
Enforcing the convict code : violence and prison culture / Rebecca Trammell.
  p. cm.
Includes bibliographical references and index.
ISBN 978-1-58826-808-2 (hc : alk. paper)
  1. Prison violence—United States. 2. Prison administration—United States.
3. Prisoners—United States. I. Title.
HV9025.T73 2012
365'.60973—dc23   2011028656

British Cataloguing in Publication Data
A Cataloguing in Publication record for this book
is available from the British Library.

Printed and bound in the United States of America

∞   The paper used in this publication meets the requirements
       of the American National Standard for Permanence of
       Paper for Printed Library Materials Z39.48-1992.

   5   4   3   2   1

To my husband,
Hoke Trammell

Contents

Acknowledgments

I am so very thankful for all of the help and support I received while writing this book. I especially want to thank my husband, Hoke, for giving me unconditional love and encouragement. I also must thank Ann Tran, Rachel Vo, Paul Backlund, Chris Hernandez, John Arthur, Jim Walsh, and Debra Kelsey; they assisted me throughout the interview process and encouraged me in countless ways. I am grateful to Valerie Jenness, Belinda Robnett, and Calvin Morrill, who gave me feedback and helped me become a better researcher. I thank my editor, Andrew Berzanskis, and the people at Lynne Rienner Publishers for their hard work on this book. Finally, I thank the brave men and women I interviewed for the book.

—*Rebecca Trammell*

1

Violence Behind Bars

In fall 2005, I was interviewing men who are members of Public Enemy Number One (PENI), a skinhead gang, in Long Beach, California. All these men had shaved heads and many tattoos, including some swastikas. Two of them had the letters "PENI" tattooed across four of their fingers. My interviewees were former inmates who agreed to meet with me to discuss their experiences in prison. I met with them in a two-bedroom home that had clearly seen better days. The walls were covered with holes, and the carpet was stained and burned in many places. Their neighborhood was full of graffiti, litter, and angry-looking pit bulls chewing at chain-link fences. These dogs charged me and barked as I walked down the street.

There was a chemical smell in the house that made me think of crystal methamphetamine, and I wondered if they were cooking meth somewhere in the house. There were two holes in the front window, and the owner claimed they were bullet holes. PENI is known for drug use and violent behavior, so none of this surprised me. Over the course of several days, I met with four men in this home and conducted lengthy interviews. I interviewed them separately, but people often interrupted us by coming in and out of the house without knocking. Also, I went with them to a community meeting for former inmates in Compton.

Each of these men told me that they were converted in prison. They said that correctional officers originally told them they would hang out only with other white men. They were approached by members of the PENI gang and told that there is strength in numbers and that they should watch their backs. They were told that black and Mexican inmates would attack them if they did not have friends. They were also warned about other skinhead groups who could not be trusted. These men joined the PENI skinhead gang and agreed to get tattooed in prison. They described people of color in racist terms and used racial stereotypes to justify their opinions. It seemed clear to me that they were angry young men. When we all met up to drive to Compton for the meeting, we had this exchange:

> LUKE: So what are you doing with these interviews?
>
> TRAMMELL: I am collecting my data to examine the causes of inmate violence. I conduct interviews with my informants and then use these interviews to show the readers what happens in prison and why.
>
> DANIEL: What the fuck did you just call us?
>
> TRAMMELL: That's just a technical term used by researchers.
>
> LUKE: We're not informants. Are we sure she's not a cop?
>
> TRAMMELL: I'm not a police officer. I'm sorry; I didn't mean that. It's really just research jargon. I can show you some books that explain what an informant is.
>
> DANIEL: I know exactly what an informant is; you can't call us informants. Judy vouched for you, and I found your information on the university website, so I think you're cool. Just watch your fucking mouth and don't ever use that term again.
>
> TRAMMELL: No problem.

As this conversation played out, I kept thinking about the fact that I was in a private home with four violent offenders, including one sex offender. I had just called them a snitch, and they were pretty angry. I also realized that spending time in prison had made them sensitive about their public identity. They were concerned about me being a police officer, but they were also concerned about being called a snitch. They brought this prison norm back into their community, along with their tattoos and opinions about people of color.

When we arrived in Compton, I had my second heart-stopping moment when I realized that I was entering a community made famous by the Crips and Bloods (African American gangs) with four skinheads. As we parked the car, Jake asked, "Are there a lot of blacks in this area?" When we all agreed that there were, Luke said, "Let's cover up," and they all put on jackets or sweatshirts to hide their tattoos. As we walked to the meeting, I asked them why they were covering up, and Luke told me: "There's no need to start trouble. We're here for a meeting, and we have you with us. Don't start trouble if you don't have to, right?" They did this to avoid conflict and protect me. They were not interested in random acts of violence. Instead, they wanted to attend their meeting in peace.

These encounters showed me how these men control their public identity. Although the gang they joined is violent, violence is not always an option. They are more than willing to get tattoos that signify their alliance to the skinhead ideology, but they are willing to cover up when necessary. Identity and reputation are very important to parolees struggling to make a life for themselves after prison. The things they learned in prison were still fresh on their minds and meaningful for them. It is entirely possible that, as time goes on, they will shed some of these behaviors and beliefs. It is also possible that they will commit another crime and go back to prison. In any event, prison has changed these men. They are now a part of a growing number of people leaving prison after the recent mass incarceration era in the United States.

In 2008, the *New York Times* reported a study conducted by the Pew Center on the States, which found that one out of every 100 adult Americans is behind bars (Liptak 2008). There are now 2.29 million people in US prisons and jails (Glaze 2010). The vast number of people entering prison since the 1980s caused problems, including overcrowded facilities, violence, and the growing drug trade in prison. The current mass incarceration trend also inspired a good deal of research focusing on these and other issues surrounding the US penal system.

For this book, I use qualitative data collected in 2005 and 2006 in California to explore how former inmates (men and women) understand and explain prison violence and inmate culture. I allow these people to explain, in their own words, the social context of inmate violence. They also explain how they often avoid violence, especially riots. Many readers will be shocked at the type and level of violence described by these men and women and by their justification of these acts as a way to control fellow inmates. They told me that violence is sometimes necessary but almost always controllable.

California is an interesting place to study prison violence. This state has one of the largest prison systems in United States. As of December 2008, there were 171,085 people incarcerated in thirty-three facilities (California Department of Corrections and Rehabilitation 2009). Also, these facilities house some of the most notorious and violent prison gangs, such as the Mexican Mafia and the Aryan Brotherhood. As others point out, racial segregation is the norm in California facilities, and gangs are racially identified (Goodman 2008; Hunt et al. 1993; Trammell 2009b). However, the US Supreme Court found that racial segregation in prison is unconstitutional; therefore, prison officials cannot separate prisoners by race (*Johnson v. California et al.* 2005). The Court's decision forced California's prison administrators to address this important issue. According to those interviewed for this book, the changes in prison policy also shocked and angered male prisoners who want racial segregation. These men often join prison gangs who fit neatly into socially constructed racial categories. In other words, this Supreme Court decision challenged the culture of racial segregation in California prisons.

Those interviewed for this book told me that forcing inmates to integrate their cells would result in mass violence, including race riots. Simply put, the men I interviewed do not want their informal norms challenged. These norms are deeply meaningful for prison inmates. While incarcerated, men use violence instrumentally as a way to maintain norms and gain power. Women interviewed for this book, conversely, state that they do not segregate by race. However, African American women were more likely to describe racial integration as beneficial for the inmates. This is just one example of how inmates describe the connection between norms, culture, and violence.

Prison Violence

Prison violence in California has been front-page news since the turn of the century (Austin 2007; Perry 2006; Risling 2006; Soto 2006; Warren 2004). Some articles focus on race riots and homicides (Austin 2007; Warren 2004), but others show how state and federal officials try to reduce violence (Perry 2006; Risling 2006; Soto 2006). For example, President George W. Bush signed the Prison Rape Elimination Act (PREA) in 2003, which details a zero tolerance policy for prison rape in the United States. Starting in 2006, the Commission on Safety and Abuse in America's Prisons collected data and held public hearings to discuss the current state of US prisons in order to make recommendations to reduce inmate violence, especially gang violence (Gibbons and Katzenbach 2006). Their report highlights the importance of safe, humane prison systems where correctional officers promote a "culture of mutual respect" in prison. They also find that prison culture cultivates violence, which puts staff and inmates at risk of harm or death:

> Growing recognition of the role that institutional culture plays in running a safe and healthy facility has led corrections administrators and other experts in the field to seek concrete ways to make positive changes in the cultures of their institutions. . . . Culture change requires ongoing efforts to shift values and behaviors over time and must be understood as a continual practice, rather than any single event or program. (67)

Overcrowded facilities and dwindling rehabilitative programs created an atmosphere in which violence is common. Members of the commission believe, and I agree, that it is possible to reverse these trends. I hope to add to this discussion by allowing parolees to explain the direct connection between violence and culture. They also explained how they tried to avoid violence and institutional reprimands. They called this "doing good time," which could be roughly defined as avoiding trouble. The term also meant that they were "good" inmates who were not stigmatized by their crimes. For example, those convicted of child molestation are "dirty" inmates who could never do good time. They live at the bottom of the prison hierarchy and are often segregated from the general population (Trammell and Chenault 2009). Those who are smart or savvy and committed a more honorable crime rise through the ranks and sometimes become informal leaders. Those who follow the "inmate code" and enforce the rules of their subculture are "solid cons," and they always do good time.

Interviewees explained that troublemakers did bad time and brought unwanted attention to the inmates. They also increase the chance of a riot, which puts the prison into a lockdown. Therefore, men and women explain that they must control these people and force them to behave for everyone's benefit. In such situations, violence is used as a method of social control. In other words, male and female inmates believe that violence does not beget violence; rather, violence prevents chaos.

Research shows that prison staff do a good job of controlling prison violence (Fleisher and Krienert 2009; Useem and Piehl 2006). In fact, Burt Useem and Anne M. Piehl (2006:107) found that the total number of riots decreased in recent years: "The data are consistent with the position that political and correctional leaders made the institution more effective." For this book, however, I explore how inmates try to control their environment by curbing the disruptive behavior of others, thus positioning the inmate as an active agent in his or her social world. Also, focusing on inmates rather than staff gives us insight into the intricacies of inmate culture.

The Culture of Total Institutions

I define "culture" as a shared set of beliefs, symbols, institutions, artifacts, values, and norms transferred from one group or generation to another. Throughout our lives, we transmit symbols that allow us to share
knowledge about our society (Charon 1998). The sociological study of
prison culture often focuses on prisons as isolated facilities (Stowell and
Byrne 2008). Prisons are a total institution (Goffman 1961) in which inmates are housed twenty-four hours per day. They must follow the rules
created by administrators; however, they develop their own informal
norms as well.

The earliest sociological work focused attention on the informal
rules created by inmates (Clemmer 1940; Hayner and Ash 1940). They
were socialized to follow a standard inmate code in which they must act
tough, not interfere with other inmates, and not befriend correctional
officers. Underground economies (i.e., dealing in cigarettes, narcotics)
developed because of a lack of social freedom. Sex, consensual or otherwise, between inmates stemmed from the lack of available women
rather than from homosexual urges (Sykes 1958). Therefore, prison violence is a byproduct of the social deprivation of incarceration (Cloward
1960; Tittle and Tittle 1964).

Later studies found that prison culture is sometimes imported from
the outside world (Irwin 1970; Irwin and Cressey 1962; Schrag 1954).
Victor Hassine (2007) argued that there is no official inmate code; inmates simply import their own norms, which are, many times, tied to
criminal activity outside prison. Research also shows a link between
street culture and prison culture, particularly with regard to drug use
and distribution (Irwin 1970) and gang activity (Moore 1991). As underground economies grew in prison, inmate culture and the inmate code
changed as some inmates used violence to maintain their businesses in
order to make money in prison (Trammell 2009b). In general, scholars
now agree that prison culture grows out of both street culture and social
deprivation; these hypotheses are not mutually exclusive (Akers,
Hayner, and Gruninger 1977; Pollock 1997; Winfree, Newbold, and
Tubb 2002). For this book, I seek to update our understanding of prison
violence and inmate culture by allowing those who lived in these facilities to explain the subtle nuances of prison norms and the social causes
of violence.

My work draws, in part, from a theoretical perspective that focuses
on culture in action (Sampson and Bean 2006; Stowell and Byrne 2008;
Swidler 1986). According to Ann Swidler (1986:284), "Within estab-

lished modes of life, culture provides a repertoire of capacities from which varying strategies of action may be constructed. Thus, culture appears to shape action only in that the cultural repertoire limits the available range of strategies of action." In other words, culture is created and shaped through an interactive process. This theory posits culture as intersubjective rather than personal (Sampson and Bean 2006). Thus, the performance is not necessarily authentic but rather is based on the expectations of the existing culture. Yet the performance is very important. According to Robert J. Sampson and Lydia Bean (2006:25): "If we adopt such a performative notion of culture, then it makes no sense to ask if 'decent' people are truly decent, and 'street' people are truly street. It makes more sense to ask which audience people are performing for and in what venues."

As previous research shows, inmate culture is shaped by the isolation of prison, and inmates carefully follow the inmate code (Sykes 1958; Terry 1997; Trammell 2009b). In this interactive process, inmates perform for other inmates and develop culture. For the inmate, cultural performances would be especially hard to avoid because prison is a total institution and they have nowhere to go. Unless they are housed in a supermax cell or live in the administrative segregation unit (solitary confinement cells), they eat, sleep, shower, and interact with each other every day.

The culture-in-action framework offers a lot to the study of inmate violence. As Jacob Stowell and James Byrne (2008:35) pointed out, "It is certainly possible that violence—both individual and collective—is more likely in situations or encounters where the 'performance of identity' is challenged in some way." Those wanting to do good time must perform their role as a solid con worthy of respect. Their behavior must align with informal norms developed and maintained by fellow inmates. Those who are able to maintain a positive identity will do much better in prison: "We need to know much more about how the symbolic violence used by individuals to carve out a 'worthy' identity (compared to some unworthy other) results in higher rates of *physical* violence in certain social contexts" (Stowell and Byrne 2008:37, emphasis in the original).

Gender and Violence

For quite some time, we knew less about incarcerated women than incarcerated men. That was, in part, due to the fact there are fewer women in prison than men; therefore, the research subject was typically male. As of December 2009, approximately 15 percent of people in prisons and jail were women. Statistically, women are more likely to be supervised in their community rather than prison (Glaze 2010). However, women are one of the fastest-growing prison populations (Blumstein and Beck 1999; Davis 2006; US Department of Justice 2005). Men commit more violent crime (sexual assault, robbery, assault, murder) than women (Federal Bureau of Investigation 2007). For example, men are almost eight times more likely to commit robbery (Renzetti 2006) and ten times more likely to commit murder (Fox and Marianne 2004; Greenfeld and Snell 1999; Renzetti 2006). Also, women are less likely to kill each other in prison (Harer and Langan 2001).

Sadly, the majority of women in prison have a history of sexual or physical abuse (57 percent), both childhood abuse and abuse that continued after they reached adulthood. Men in prison report less childhood abuse (14 percent); 5.8 percent of male inmates were abused as adults (Chesney-Lind 2002). Clearly, there are some differences between male and female inmates. In this book, I examine the similarities and differences in men's and women's descriptions of inmate culture and violence. I do so for several reasons. First, although there is evidence that some women hurt each other in prison (Alarid 2000; Greer 2000; Trammell 2009a), many researchers tend to focus on men because, quite frankly, they are more likely to commit violence. Women in my study mostly denounced violence as something that "men do." However, they also described acts of physical and sexual violence but minimized the harm done by violence by blaming the victim. In this sense, their stories were very similar to those of their male counterparts. Men sought to control others who were bringing unwanted attention to their activities. Women did that as well but often blamed women for breaching gender norms. In other words, the rules of gender are strictly enforced. Men described a hypermasculine environment, whereas women described behaving in a civilized manner. In either case, fellow inmates often controlled those who strayed outside their assigned gender roles.

Second, I compare men and women because doing so broadens our theoretical understanding about the behaviors of US inmates. As Jody Miller (2001:3) pointed out:

> For over a century, theories developed to explain why people commit crime have actually been theories of why men commit crime. Some contemporary scholars have thus been keen on the question of whether, or to the extent that, these theories can explain women's par-

ticipation in crime. Moreover, feminist scholars have posed the question: can the logic of such theories be modified to include women?

Historically, research on masculinity and crime ignored girls and women and used (the male) gender as a predictor of crime and violence. That approach "neglects the fact that women and girls occasionally engage in masculine practices and crime, and therefore constructs a transparent dualist criminology" (Messerschmidt 2006:29–30). Here, James W. Messerschmidt built on the work of R. W. Connell (2000), who argued that crime and violence are expressed (by men or women) as masculine traits. However, Messerschmidt called for going beyond a "dualist criminological" approach to understanding interpersonal violence. If violence is constructed as "masculine" behavior, we come to believe that there is something seriously wrong with violent women, which affects the type and level of punishment women receive. For example, L. Kay Gillespie (2000:126) found that women who are executed in the United States often "fail to portray the expected gender role of a woman." In other words, women who do not appear matronly or gentle have a higher chance of being sentenced to death.

Although men are more likely to commit violent crime, criminological studies now focus on both men and women. According to Messerschmidt (2006:29), "Not only is the importance of gender to understanding crime more broadly acknowledged within the discipline, but also it has led, logically, to the critical study of masculinity and crime. Boys and men are no longer seen as the 'normal subjects'; rather, the social construction of masculinities has come under careful criminological scrutiny." Overall, I found that women often compared their experiences to those of men. They said that they knew how men acted in prison and would tell me how their behavior was similar to or different from what men do. Yet, when I asked the men in my study if they knew what happened in women's prisons, they would often laugh or tell me that it was a stupid question. They explained that they had no idea what went on in women's prisons, nor did they care.

Third, interviewees also discussed the Hollywood version of prison life and compared their experiences to things portrayed in movies and on television. Of course, movies often show prison from a male perspective. Movies consistently portray violence and other criminal behaviors as acceptable masculine behavior (Eschholz and Bufkin 2001). In examining prison movies from the 1990s, O'Sullivan (2006:496) found that "In these films, women are either conspicuous by their absence and/or used in entirely conventional ways." Certainly, there is no shortage of movies and television shows that focus on men in prison. For example, one of the more famous prison shows, *Oz* (which aired from 1997 to 2003), often depicted the brutal behavior of men living in a prison in New York. Those interviewed discussed these cultural references and told me that fictional stories about prison are exaggerated and mostly false.

What I find particularly interesting is the fact that women compared their experiences to men. The women in my study constantly explained how they were better and more civilized but were treated badly. There are several reasons why women made these comparisons. First, it is highly likely that these women felt stigmatized by their prison record and wanted to maintain a positive identity. In fact, they often told me that they were treated badly in and out of prison because they were women. Many claimed that judges yelled at them for being bad mothers, and almost all of them stated that they had a hard time getting a job because of their criminal record. They could distance themselves from the harsh stigma of incarceration by explaining that female inmates are not violent.

Second, they believed that the criminal justice system was not designed for women, especially mothers. They stated that they were not given enough rehabilitative services in prison because those programs were reserved for men. In 2005, the California Department of Corrections and Rehabilitation (CDCR) was put under federal receivership because of the lack of medical care in California prisons. A federal class action lawsuit, *Plata v. Schwarzenegger* (2001) was brought against the prison system, alleging that the lack of medical care violated the Eighth Amendment. Federal judges put the prison under federal receivership in order to bring the system up to appropriate standards. The fact that women, and some men, stated that they were not adequately taken care of in prison was not an exaggeration. However, one key difference was that women blamed men for using resources they wanted. Men, however, often told me that they had no interest in prison programs.

The Inmate Perspective

For this book, I allowed interviewees to describe these issues from their perspectives. This method humanizes them and helps us to examine how the inmates construct reality. Of course, giving them such free rein brought up questions about the accuracy and honesty of their statements. It was possible that they would downplay their own behavior or lie about their experiences. However, I found that men and women were quite willing to talk about their life in prison. They described all sorts of violent acts they witnessed or committed in prison, then explained how experiencing violence was the normal prison experience. Moreover, violence was sometimes described as the only way to get justice or peace in prison. In this sense, violence symbolized strength and power in an environment where they have no real, legitimate power.

I do not know if they were always completely honest with me, but I think that they believed the stories they told. They often told me that violence was not the biggest problem in prison. Instead, they listed the bad food and lack of medical and dental care as the real problems. I should note that most of the terms they used, such as "cellie" (cellmate/roommate), "shot-callers" (gang leaders), and "guards" or "cops" (correctional officers) were universal. Their description of correctional officers as lazy, sadistic, or stupid was mostly universal. No former inmates described correctional officers as hard working, but several women described them as good Christian men who were just trying to do their job. All the men in this study described correctional officers as lazy and dumb.

They may, by accident or deliberate action, have given me inaccurate statements. However, the interview process allowed me to question them in several ways. The interviewees were able to describe, in their own words, what happens in prison and to talk about the meanings behind the actions they committed or witnessed (Blumer 1969). As others point out, qualitative methods allow the reader to understand the reality of those with a deviant or stigmatized identity (Blee 2002; Miller 2001; Polsky 2006; Simi 2010; Snow and Anderson 1993). In this sense, their reality was their own, and their descriptions were accurate from their perspective.

Methodology

For my study, I examined how former inmates understand violence as a social process. I defined violence as any structured arrangement that results in physical or nonphysical harm, as defined by Peter Iadicola and Anson Shupe (2003). For a researcher, a direct observation of inmate violence is impossible. Prisons are closed institutions, and researchers rarely gain access to California inmates. Therefore, I interviewed former California inmates and allowed them to describe the social process of violence as well as inmate culture. I used open-ended interview questions

(Denzin and Lincoln 1998) that allowed my interviewees to thoroughly explain how they understood violence and inmate culture. I made primary contact at reentry programs and parole meetings in Southern California. (See Tables 1.1 and 1.2.)

Using a snowball technique, in which I relied on inmates who were willing to meet with me and be interviewed, I interviewed them in public places and private homes. I used pseudonyms to protect their identity and privacy. Tables 1.1 and 1.2 include their age, race, crime committed, and time served. I intentionally left these details out of the narrative so that the reader can focus on the person rather than the crime each committed.

In many qualitative studies, interviewees are called "informants" (Duneier 2001). As previously mentioned, my interviewees asked me not to use this term because it is synonymous with the term "snitch," a pejorative term used by inmates and parolees. Therefore, I used the term "interviewee" throughout this book. Interviews lasted approximately one to two hours and were tape-recorded and transcribed verbatim. Responses were coded by gender to specifically examine differences and similarities in responses. I interviewed a total of seventy-three parolees. The average age is thirty-three years old. They served prison sentences in medium- to maximum-security facilities in California, and their sentences ranged from eighteen months to fifteen years.

Because this book is qualitative in nature, I do not claim to offer the exact number of violent offenses in prison or the rates or prevalence of prison violence. Instead, I give those with firsthand knowledge a chance to explain how and why violence happens behind bars, allowing the reader to understand the nuances of inmate culture and violence. The interviewees described the conditions under which violence occurred in terms that are sometimes shocking. Many times, interviewees described race, gender, and violence in a way that would offend those of us who have not lived or worked in prison, which is a closed society with its own distinct culture. At the same time, inmates take their own values and norms into prison, so this culture is not created in a vacuum. It would be easy to dismiss or demonize their culture because they are all convicted felons. We see news stories about prison riots and come to the conclusion that these people behave badly because they are bad people. However, living in a total institution creates an environment in which people often act out against those who control them.

As we learned in the famous Zimbardo/Stanford prison experiment, "good" men who had no criminal history took on the role of the "prisoner" and, within days, began acting out (Zimbardo 2008; Zimbardo et

Table 1.1 Male Interviewees

Age	Pseudonym	Race	Offense(s)	Time Served
28	Jose	Hispanic	Aggravated assault, parole violation	3 years
32	Juan	Hispanic	Robbery and assault	7 years
39	Ramon	Hispanic	Robbery	5 years
36	Carlos	Hispanic	Attempted murder	5 years
32	Martino	Hispanic	Domestic violence/battery	3 years
22	Oscar	Hispanic	Drug possession	18 months
34	James	Black	Manslaughter	8 years
35	Eduardo	Hispanic	Grand theft auto, assault, robbery	8 years
32	Rey	Hispanic	Grand theft auto, drug possession	2 years
33	Adam	White	Drug possession, parole violation	3 years
36	Seth	White	Drug possession and burglary	16 months
40	Chuck	White	Parole violation	9 months
38	Max	White	Drug possession, assault, robbery	4 years
30	Luke	White	Assault with a deadly weapon, sexual battery, and robbery	5 years
45	Samuel	Black	Robbery, drugs	13 years
32	Austin	White	Drunk driving, absconding	1 year
24	Luis	Hispanic	Robbery and grand theft auto	8 years
28	Roberto	Hispanic	Robbery and assault	6 years
46	Roman	Hispanic	Robbery and assault	5 years
29	Ian	White	Robbery, rape one—adult	10 years
33	Daniel	White	Assault, attempted murder	10 years
37	Jake	White	Grand theft auto, sexual assault, car jacking	15 years
29	Vincent	White	Assault, sexual assault	11 years
30	Bobby	White	Robbery	8 years
40	Miguel	Hispanic	Robbery	5 years
35	Geraldo	Hispanic	Drug trafficking and attempted murder	9 years
35	Gil	Hispanic	Manslaughter	15 years
29	Anthony	White	Parole violation, assault	2 years
42	Angelo	Black	Drugs, assault, attempted murder	6 years
30	Ethan	Black	Robbery	5 years
36	Daryl	Black	Robbery	4 years
30	Evan	White	Robbery, sexual assault	7 years
26	Aiden	White	Robbery	4 years
36	Ronald	Black	Drug trafficking, robbery	7 years
35	Tyler	White	Robbery and assault	8 years
29	Kory	White	Aggravated assault, attempted murder	5 years
40	Brad	Black	Drug trafficking, assault	6 years
39	Hal	Black	Aggravated assault, kidnapping	12 years
41	Pedro	Hispanic	Drugs, burglary	2 years
32	Leon	Hispanic	Robbery and assault	6 years

Table 1.2 Female Interviewees

Age	Pseudonym	Race	Offense(s)	Time Served
30	Ella	Black	Drug possession	4 years
45	Emma	White	Drug trafficking	1 year
36	Stella	White	Drug possession	18 months
40	Julia	White	Drug possession	18 months
45	Bella	Hispanic	Drug trafficking	18 months
32	Molly	Black	Assault and battery	1 year
40	Judy	White	Attempted murder	28 months
28	Polly	White	Drug possession and prostitution	16 months
32	Olivia	White	Drug possession and trafficking	4 years
34	Marilyn	White	Drug possession	16 months
30	Leah	White	Embezzlement and drug possession	16 months
31	Caroline	White	Drug possession	16 months
28	Joanne	Black	Drug trafficking	16 months
36	Karla	Black	Drug possession and aggravated assault	4 years
27	Hayley	Black	Assault and battery	18 months
30	Alexandria	Black	Burglary, drug possession, parole violation	3 years
30	Prudence	Black	Domestic violence and drug possession	4 years
30	Aura	Hispanic	Parole violation and drug possession	2 years
33	Rosa	Hispanic	Embezzlement and drug possession	2 years
27	Sofia	White	Assault w/deadly weapon and drug possession	16 months
45	Lupe	Hispanic	Drug possession	9 months
31	Barbara	White	Drug possession	16 months
37	Rita	Hispanic	Drugs, robbery, and parole violation	9 years
31	Edith	Biracial, black, white	Drugs, domestic abuse	2 years
34	Stephanie	White	Drugs, embezzlement	2 years
32	Rosario	Hispanic	Attempted murder	6 years
43	Charlotte	White	Drug violation and parole violation	6 years
30	Hannah	White	Drug possession	6 years
31	Emily	White	Drug possession, robbery	8 years
43	Lucy	White	Drugs, parole violation	2 years
26	Mia	White	Drugs, parole violation	3 years
40	Lauren	White	Drugs	9 months
34	Tina	White	Drugs	18 months

al. 1974). Philip Zimbardo carefully screened each of his participants, and only the "best" men (i.e., no drug use, no history of violence) were allowed to participate in his experiment. Each man was randomly assigned the role of guard or prisoner. Prisoners were locked in a jail, and the guards were told they had to control them. Within two days, inmates and guards became hostile, and some prisoners had emotional breakdowns. Some of the guards became sadistic toward the inmates, while other (nonsadistic) guards looked the other way. None of these men were actually inmates or guards. Instead, they accepted their roles and used their limited knowledge of inmate culture to guide their behavior.

Zimbardo concluded that social context is important (Zimbardo 2008). Under the right circumstances, many of us would act out or use violence to achieve some goal. Of course, his conclusion does not excuse bad behavior. It simply puts it in context. We lock up people for breaking the law and expect them to behave in a civilized manner. Moreover, we somehow expect them to learn from their experiences and become better people. I am sure that many people believe that incarceration reduces crime. Yet here is no evidence that harsh punishment, alone, prevents crime.

One question every American should ask is, what do inmates learn from each other? It is highly likely that people go into prison as convicted felons and leave as something else. They may leave as better people who saw the error of their ways, or they may have learned better ways to commit crime. They may have been rehabilitated, or they may have been victimized, terrorized, or turned into violent predators. Over 90 percent of inmates are returned to their communities (Petersilia 2003). Another question Americans should ask is, what type of person do I want standing next to me in the grocery store? Do I want that person to have access to rehabilitation programs in prison? Perhaps he learned to read and write or gained some valuable work skills. Or do I want that person to have suffered long-term physical or sexual abuse in prison? Do I want her to have kicked her drug or alcohol addiction or to have joined a prison gang? As we filled prisons beyond capacity and reduced the number of prison programs, very few people asked themselves these questions. I personally worry about who we release back into our communities. I would hope that everyone worries about that. To answer some of these questions, I allowed these men and women the opportunity to explain how inmates behave in prison and what they learn from inmate culture.

There are some limitations to this method that the reader should understand. At the time of data collection, there were over 161,000 inmates in California prisons; therefore, these data are not generalizable to the entire prison population. In fact, quantitative prison research data are best for examining the decline of prison riots (Useem and Piehl 2006). Furthermore, I used a snowball sample rather than a randomized sample; relying on inmates who were willing to meet with me means that my sample does not represent all inmates in California. Finally, a direct observation of violence is optimal. However, I focused on the accounts and justifications told by former inmates. In other words, I relied on their memory of violent events and social interactions.

On the positive side, this method allowed interviewees to elaborate on my questions. Furthermore, quantitative methods do not effectively allow the researcher into the socially constructed world of the research subject. Specifically, I focused on the narratives, or more specifically, the "plot lines" (Burck 2005; Reissman 1993) of these narratives. Their narratives told a story from beginning to end. They highlighted the subjective reality of people or social groups who wanted to explain their social world. They gave interviewees a voice to describe and deconstruct social reality from their vantage point.

Chapter Overview

In Chapter 2, I explore prison culture from the perspective of former inmates. They discuss how they learned to behave like typical inmates. I found that they mentor new inmates in order to get them to acclimate to prison culture. This allows them to maintain their own informal norms in prison and gives them some power over their own lives. In Chapter 3, interviewees describe race relations in California prisons. There is ample evidence that men segregate by race in California prisons and create gangs along racial lines (Goodman 2008; Hunt et al. 1993; Trammell 2009b). However, some of the women in my study also described racial conflict between inmates. White and Hispanic women are more likely to want segregation, and many women described fighting about race. In addition, men have some friends of different races, and many claimed that they had no problems with race in prison.

In Chapter 4, I focus on how former inmates describe sex and rape in prison. Both men and women often describe prison as a hypersexual environment. They explain that those who dominate their partners often occupy a masculine role in these relationships. Men and women who embrace a hypermasculine identity gain power by doing so. Also, women claim that some women abuse their girlfriends. In Chapter 5, interviewees describe how they deal with daily problems. Their methods were greatly influenced by both prison culture and gender norms. Both men and women approached these problems in a way that maintained or raised their own social status. Men usually fought someone to put him in his place. Women tried to outsmart each other, spread rumors, and avoid problem inmates. In any event, their methods lined up nicely with prescribed gender roles.

In Chapter 6, interviewees describe the mechanisms of social control. Drawing from my interviews, it seems as if formal controls work better for women than men. Women described following instructions, whereas men bragged about breaking the rules. There is little doubt that prescribed gender norms dictate that women should be less physically aggressive than men (Cahill 1989; Connell 1987, 2000; Thorne 1998). To be sure, that is one reason why women do not fight as much as men. However, women claimed to have received written reprimands for less serious offenses that served as a reminder that they were being watched. Men, however, create rituals that help them avoid interacting with prison staff. I conclude in Chapter 7 with a discussion about gender, social control, and inmate culture. I also discuss how prison officials can help maintain a culture of mutual respect in their prison facilities.

2

Prison Culture

Most people probably believe that prison is a frightening and depressing place where rape is common and many people die. Movies and television shows often depict this institution as dysfunctional and violent. Almost every prison movie includes a violent rape scene, and correctional officers are portrayed as sadistic, uncaring, or incompetent. To some degree, these stereotypes affect our worldview about incarceration. Those interviewed for my study often told me that prison is nothing like what we see on television or in the movies. In fact, they explained that prison is usually boring. Inmates often had jobs (work duty) and spent a lot of time playing cards, watching television, or hanging out in the prison yard. They told me that the fictional accounts of prison are exactly that, fictional. However, violence does occur in this institution, and there is no shortage of data on prison violence.

If inmates are caught fighting, they receive a California Department of Corrections and Rehabilitation written violation, called a CDCR 115, or "115" for short. This reprimand impacts their "good time" credit. They are charged with "mutual combat" or "assault," depending on whether two people fight or one person attacks another (California Department of Corrections and Rehabilitation 2003). Officials document these incidents to compile state reports about violence, homicides, and other crimes committed in prison.

Official, public reports from the California Department of Corrections and Rehabilitation show that, from 1997 to 2006, an average of thirteen men died each year because of an assault, battery, or escape (California Department of Corrections and Rehabilitation 2007). These same reports show that, on average, twenty-eight inmates (males and females combined) committed suicide each year. Since 1980, a total of four employees (three correctional officers and one factory supervisor) were killed by inmates in California state prisons (California Department of Corrections and Rehabilitation 2008b). On average, there were 2,931 assaults on prison staff each year in California prisons (California Department of Corrections and Rehabilitation 2006a). The most common form of violence is assaults between inmates, with an average of 4,902 assaults without a weapon and 2,086 assaults with a weapon each year. The number of reported assaults varies widely by gender. Women commit 304 documented assaults each year on average, and men commit 6,684 assaults on average (California Department of Corrections and Rehabilitation 2006a).

These are reported assaults; we can assume that some fights or assaults are not reported to prison officials. Also, bias or inconsistencies could exist in how officials document and report violent behavior (Sumner and Matsuda 2006). Yet these reports tell us several things. First, more inmates commit suicide each year than die from being assaulted. Also, assaults between inmates without a weapon are the most frequently reported type of violence in California prisons.

Rape and sexual assaults are rarely reported in US prisons. At the national level, inmate surveys show that 4.4 percent of prison inmates and 3.1 percent of jail inmates report being sexually assaulted (Beck et al. 2010). In California, a research team from the University of California collected data in 2006 in response to the federal Prison Rape Elimination Act (2003). They interviewed a random sample of male inmates in six adult prisons ($N = 322$). They also interviewed a nonrandom sample of transgender inmates. Transgender inmates were "identified either through self-identification, identification of related medical records (i.e., hormonal treatment), or participation in groups for transgender inmates" (Jenness et al. 2007:16).

The research team contacted all identified transgender inmates at one prison and interviewed 94 percent of them ($N = 39$) for their study (Jenness et al. 2007:2). They found that 37 percent of non-transgender California male inmates reported never experiencing any form of violence in prison (54). They also found that 4 percent of non-transgender inmates reported being raped, and 1.3 percent engaged in a sexual act that they did not want to do (27). Within their random sample, 58 percent of male inmates reported being nonsexually assaulted (30). For the transgender (nonrandom) sample, 59 percent reported being sexually assaulted, and 16 percent reported being nonsexually assaulted in prison (Jenness et al. 2007:27).

Transgender inmates reported that prison staff were aware of only 29 percent of the assaults against them and that 64 percent of these victims received no medical attention (Jenness et al. 2007: 37). Conversely, 70 percent of non-transgender inmates who were sexually assaulted received medical attention, and prison staff was aware of 61 percent of these attacks (Jenness et al. 2007:37). Statistically, those who are at risk of sexual assault are men with mental health problems or small physical statures and those who are African American or transgender (Jenness et al. 2007:33).

This research indicates that, for non-transgendered inmates, rape is rarely reported. Of course, it is likely that some violent acts go unreported. Mark Fleisher and Jessie Keinert (2009) argue that inmates create their own definitions of rape with a narrow scope. In other words, if inmates do not define behavior as rape, they will not report being raped. Rape stories, or "myths," are common in prison to warn inmates about the dangers of owing someone money or favors. At the same time, violent acts of rape are downplayed if the victim receives some kind of compensation (safety, money, drugs) in return for sexual favors (Fleisher and Krienert 2009).

There are several problems with collecting data on prison rape.

> Personal interviews of inmates have generally yielded low positive response rates (below 1 percent). These low rates of reporting do not permit further analyses of victim, perpetrator, and facility characteristics. More recent studies with self-administered questionnaires have yielded higher prevalence rates (around 20 percent with a broad definition of sexual assault). However, the credibility of such studies remains in question due to low questionnaire completion rates (e.g., 25 percent response rate) and loss of control over who completes the forms and under what settings. (Beck, Harrison, and Hughes 2004:2)

Due to the fact that surveys and personal interviews yielded a low prevalence rate, the US Bureau of Justice is using computer-assisted personal interviewing and audio computer-assisted self-interviewing to evaluate the prevalence of prison rape. These studies yielded the current finding of 4.4 percent of prison inmates nationwide reporting sexual assault (Beck et al. 2010).

I want to remind the reader that I did not use national data for this book. Also, I am not examining the prevalence of sexual or nonsexual assaults in prison. Instead, I used qualitative data that allowed former inmates to explain violent behavior from their perspective. My goal was to understand how violence is linked to cultural norms in prison. Violence, as a cultural artifact, is often facilitated by structural inequalities built into every institution (Iadicola and Shupe 2003). We create categories such as race, gender, and class and then create social hierarchies based on these categories that make some people deserving of violence. Prison is no exception: inmates create social categories and often join gangs or cliques fueled by in-group alliances.

I discuss these recent data on prison violence to highlight the fact that prisons are controlled environments (Useem and Piehl 2006). Inmates who are sexually assaulted now have highly trained personnel to help them report what happened and get help (Fleisher and Krienert 2009). This is not to say that prisons are safe, violence-free spaces. The men and women in my study described a good deal of violence, but they often minimized the harm that violence caused. They described prison norms, including norms about violence, as grounded in rational, moral decisions. All the men in my study claimed that they, rather than prison staff, controlled problem inmates.

Maintaining a Worthy Identity in Men's Prisons

Some of the men in my study explained why it was important to control each other in prison. They also stated that it was important to appear tough and masculine. Martino described the connection between masculine traits and social control:

> MARTINO: In prison, it's about fronting. You have to show the others that you are tough or you won't survive. But, you know what? There are some messed-up guys in prison. These guys will cut you or sell you out. I had to take some of these guys down a notch or two. A lot of [the] time, you get a guy inside who is out of control, you know, he can't control himself so we had to check them. We would send someone to put them in check. If they keep that shit up, we all pay. The guards will crawl up our ass and they could start a riot. I would say that, a lot of times, we had to keep everyone in line.
>
> TRAMMELL: Don't the officers do that?
>
> MARTINO: No, they can't see half the shit that goes on. They don't know dick about this stuff. We knew exactly where to go to fight and how to get away with it. We wanted to control the boys, so we did.

Oscar explained how he put on a show for the correctional officers and then did whatever he wanted in the yard or the cells:

The cops are mostly union guys; they just want to do their job and go home. The less they do, the happier they are. If you give them more work, they get pissed. The trick is to give them as little as possible to do, and run the show. We would act all nice to them, get them to take one of their union breaks and then do whatever the hell we want. If you can get them to ignore you, you're golden. I would act like a perfect gentleman in front of them, show respect and say "yes sir, no sir" and then sell my stuff on the yard or take down a guy who was dissing me in his cell. You have to know when and where to start shit and when to mellow out.

Several men discussed the correctional officers union, which is a powerful labor union in California. Interviewees claimed that the union protects officers so they can do little work and still get paid. Almost all the people in this study believed that correctional officers do as little work as possible. In reality, prison staff are well trained to handle disruptions and violence (Useem and Piehl 2006). Yet former inmates asserted that they took control of their own environment. I do not mean to say that they are lying or making up stories. It may very well be true that some correctional officers do as little work as necessary while inmates sell drugs and run other businesses. In fact, underground economies, such as the drug trade, are such a problem that in 2005 federal prosecutors arrested and prosecuted gang members in California prisons under the Racketeer Influenced and Corrupt Organizations (RICO) Act (Risling 2006). At the same time, it is safe to assume that correctional officers and other staff work very hard to control inmates and maintain a peaceful environment.

Some men explained how they manipulated their environment in prison by putting on a show. They showed the correctional officers respect while selling drugs or assaulting other inmates. Max describes this performance:

You know, you have to follow all the rules of the institution and stuff, you know you have to do what the COs tell you and there's all this shit you have to do about what to do and when to do it, but the guys in the yard also tell you do . . . what your own people tell you. It's a game: you have the official rules, no going out of bounds and stuff, but there are the rules of the yard and the rules of the cell. We knew when to fight and when not to. You know, there are riots in prison, but those are planned and we know when to let things go. You get confused about all the rules at first, but the longer you are in, the easier it is. At first, I got in a lot of fights cuz some guy would stare me down or say shit to me; then I learned the rules, and I knew when to ignore shit and when to pay attention. The longer you are there, the easier it is. You just have to learn when and where to do your thing.

Others explained how they had different performances for different audiences. Juan stated that inmates could not lie to fellow gang members, but it was acceptable to lie to prison staff:

> It's about being real for the boys. You can't say or do whatever in front of the cops. We know how to act in front of them. If you lie to them, it's not a big deal. You just have to be straight with your boys. I knew this guy who was pretty dumb, and he would say shit to the guards, just run his mouth off. We had to tell him, "Hey, don't talk to them, don't give them anything." It's best to say nothing to them or ignore them. If you start saying shit to them, they may think something is up, and they'll get in our business. If you ignore them, everyone is happy. If you are smart, you figure this out right away. The problem is, not a lot of guys in prison are smart.

They also confirmed that they could not go to the prison staff for help. It was important to maintain some distance from the correctional officers. Max stated:

> They [correctional officers] are pretty dumb. I mean, they don't know much, I guess some of them are okay. I just didn't deal with them. You know you don't ever want anyone to think that you are in cahoots with him or her. The best thing you can do is avoid them. You can't ever complain to them. It's not like I can say, "Hey, Smith, that guy's bothering me, make him stop," right? That's never going to happen. If that happens, you're dead. So the best you can do is avoid. I got a black eye once, from a fight, and they asked what happened, and I told them I ran into a door. They kept joking that this is what abused women say when their man beats them. They were trying to get to me by saying that I'm a chick. Whatever, I let it roll off of me, man, screw those guys. They can't make me say shit.

These men outlined three basic rules about prison culture: (1) they must quickly learn the informal norms to stay out of trouble; (2) there is a time and place for violence, and the trick is to learn when and where to fight; and (3) their behavior is described as a performance. In fact, they performed for the correctional officers and for each other. Martino explained that inmates must "front," which meant putting up a persona of toughness or hypermasculinity. They cannot appear weak or subservient in front of other inmates. Doing so puts them at risk for victimization. They might, however, put up a polite front to the correctional officers, but that was just an act. They had to convince prison staff that everything was fine in order to keep them at bay.

The Socialization Process

Most of us are socialized to know what behavior is appropriate in different social settings. The way we act with our friends will be dramatically different from how we act with colleagues or relatives. According to Erving Goffman (1959), social interactions are "performances" taking place between actors. This idea is rooted in what Goffman calls the interaction order, which takes place during face-to-face encounters (Goffman 1959, 1983). It dictates the behavior between actors and how behavior is understood by all the participants. We do not simply act for the sake of acting; the performance is carried out to maintain a desired impression of the self.

Inmates described having two audiences. They maintained a worthy public identity to fellow inmates if they acted tough and in control. They kept correctional staff out of their way if they reduced conflict. The overlapping element was control. No one wanted to break up a fight or tend to injured inmates. Thus inmates and staff had a common goal, which was to reduce conflict and violence. For inmates, reducing violence meant stopping or redirecting it in a way that was not visible to the staff. Either way, both groups got what they wanted by keeping violence hidden from the staff.

Culture is shaped through an interactive process (Sampson and Bean 2006; Stowell and Byrne 2008; Swidler 1986). The performance is not necessarily grounded in realistic or authentic beliefs or situations, but rather, the performance draws from cultural expectations. These men described the conflict between inmate and correctional officer as a fight for control. The social setting of prison limited the available strategies of action. In reality, inmates could change very little about their environment. They could not leave, gain legitimate control of the prison, or change official rules. They were disenfranchised and weak. Therefore, if they gained any real power, they did so through informal social networks.

Of course, cultural expectations about inmate behavior influenced how prisoners respond to conflict. Their choices of action were also affected by gender norms. In this sense, violence was a logical choice. Violence is socially constructed as a masculine behavior. Those who study gender have shown how young boys create a pecking order within their social groups and use aggression to rise up in the pecking order (Cahill 1989; Eder, Evans, and Parker 1997; Thorne 1993). Moreover, violence is sometimes used to dominate others (Bourdieu 2001; Connell 1987,

2000). These men described how they "put someone in check" or "take someone down" in order to control disruptive behavior.

The Mexican Mafia is one of the oldest prison gangs in the United States. They are often called La Eme, which is the pronunciation of the letter "M" in the Spanish alphabet. Interviewees explain that the terms "Southerner" or "Sureños" refer to Mexican gangs from Southern California. Southern gangs include the Mexican Mafia or those aligned with this powerful prison gang. "Northerners" or "Norteños" are Mexican gangs from Northern California, including La Nuestra Familia (Our Family). The Mexican Mafia and La Nuestra Familia are rival gangs.

Ramon, who identified as a "Southerner," told me how important it is for men in prison to be honest with gang members:

> You have to be connected. If you pretend to be a gang member and we find out you're not, you get hurt. We'll punk you out or take you out. We check things; you have to have the right connections, you know what I mean? No posers in the gang. Look, we got the numbers inside; we organize and think smart. We give people the rules in writing; our boys learn from us and follow the rules. You won't make it a day if you don't follow our rules.

One way to maintain control is to make sure that everyone follows informal rules. According to Jose, gangs work to organize their behavior: "We set up a structure in prison. In fact, in some prisons, like in San Quentin, La Eme [the Mexican Mafia gang] has a handbook, you know, like a written book on rules and regulations. The COs spend a lot of time up there confiscating the book. They're such assholes; those books keep us in line. It tells us what to do and what we can't do." In other words, if inmates know the rules, there will be fewer fights. These men describe how they organize their gangs by race.

Table 2.1 shows the demographics of inmates by race. According to these CDCR reports, approximately 38 percent of male inmates are Hispanic, 29 percent are African American, and 27 percent are white (California Department of Corrections and Rehabilitation 2008a). Hispanic men are the majority race in California prisons, and their gangs are some of the oldest. There are "Border Brothers," men who were born in Mexico or South America. They are not identified as American gang members. They often try to join gangs in prison, but interviewees stated that they never became gang leaders because they were not "real Chicano" men; they were Mexican. In other words, they discriminated against these men because of their immigration status. African American gangs (such as the Crips and Bloods) are also prevalent, and over the last forty years,

Table 2.1 Race and Gender in California Prisons, 2006

	Men	Women
White	43,714	4,534
Black	45,982	3,354
Hispanic	61,610	3,238
Other	9,466	610

Source: California Department of Corrections and Rehabilitation. 2006b.

skinhead gangs have mobilized in California prisons (Hunt et al. 1993; Irwin 1980). I point this out to illustrate how men organize their gangs. There are so many gangs in California prisons that race is not the only dividing characteristic. Region, immigration status, and gang affiliation outside prison also matter.

Race is a major cause of inmate violence for male inmates (Jenness et al. 2007). The norms surrounding racial segregation influence the way men organize their lives and control each other. Luke explained how men segregate:

> I'm a white guy, so I can only hang with white guys in prison. The COs told me that I would only run with the white guys. I knew that going in, but they told me too. A guy, a white guy, came up to me right away and told me to get with the skins and I'd be okay. I got some ink, some white power stuff, and I'd only hang with my cars [fellow gang members]. I guess that the other guys, the black guys, get the same treatment, so they know what's up. I think the wetbacks do a lot more formal things; they make guys prove they were in their gangs back on the streets, we didn't go that far. There are not a lot of white guys in prison, so we could not spend a lot of time checking references, right? It was very clear; everyone knows the rules; it's not hard to figure out.

It is interesting to note that, although men described racial segregation as the norm, they often told me how other gangs are organized. Luke, for example, described how Mexican gangs made sure that new gang members were connected to gangs outside prison. Ronald told me this story:

> We talk, and there are no secrets about who sells what and who is up to something. I remember these Mexican guys once told me that they knew the white guys were going to start shit with us over something. How did they know that? We talk to each other. They told us this; now we owe them, right? This does not mean that we are friends but knowledge is power, you know?

Interviewees explained that they knew who to go to for information or drugs or anything else. Of course, nothing is free: Ronald now owes this other gang for this information. Fleisher and Krienert (2009) point out that it is dangerous to owe something to inmates in prison. My interviewees often explained that, although they worked hard to avoid drug debts and other favors, they shared a good deal of information and traded favors under many circumstances. Of course, there were clear rules about who communicated with whom. For example, Jake explained how information is shared:

> I was PENI [skinhead gang], so I hung out with my boys. If I need to talk with some black guy or something, my boys know this and have my back. Let's say that they owe us money or something. My leader tells me to talk with their Lieutenant and set up the rules. There's really no problem here, and no one is jumping me or anything. It would be a lot worse if I did not know what was going on with the brothers, you know? We have to talk. I remember this one time, the colored guys owed us some money, so I go to their guys and say, "Hey, man, I want to work with you, but I'm not a punk, you need to pay up." They were totally cool, their guy was like, "That's cool man, I get it, we'll talk with the boys." Stuff like that. I have to tell you, I do not like the blacks; I know that's not cool, but I don't like them. That doesn't mean that I won't talk to them. If the time is right and they owe me money, they will pay up if I explain that it's about business. Everyone is fine with that.

I asked him about fighting, and he told me this story: "I took down this mouthy nigger once. He was a new guy and didn't know that he should respect me. I don't think that he had any friends yet and he took one look at me and my boys and started talking shit. I smacked him around and showed him how we roll. Like I said, I don't like the colored guys so I had no problem doing this." Ian, another member of the PENI skinhead gang, had this to say:

> The black dudes were slow at training their new guys. When they come in, we have a talk and set them straight. My boys were on it; you cannot fuck around and let this slide. The Mexicans, they know what's what and they were quick, but the black guys, that's a different story. I had to remind them several times, you know, "You have a new boy on the yard" and stuff. They are some lazy people, I tell you.

Inmates felt they had to work fast to socialize the new inmates. They would make contact with new inmates and inform them of the rules. James told me how it was done:

JAMES: I told you, I ran with the Crips, right? Well, we had lots of guys in prison who are racist, plain and simple. These guys, they will say shit to you and call names and stuff. Well, some of our guys, the young ones, will get pissed about that. They are not taking that racist shit from anyone. Okay, so we would have to talk to them, tell them, look, I'm a lot older than you, I know what's up. You can't freak out every time you hear the word "nigger," right? You can talk with the leaders if you want to fight, that's fine, but you cannot just jump a guy in the yard.

TRAMMELL: Why not?

JAMES: That's bad; now we have a riot. The guards will see that something is up and they'll start watching us, and I don't blame them for that. That's their job, right? But you start bringing down another guy, and now everyone is involved and it's a mess. So I say, look, talk to the leaders, see if they'll let you take the guy down in a blind spot or in their cell. Keep that shit low-key, right? No need to bring in the cops over some name calling. We can take care of that.

Kory told me how other PENI members helped him understand the informal rules:

When I got in, the other guys took me under their wing. They showed me where to go and what to do. They explained how to act in the yard and in front of the other guys. You know, you have to front to the Peckerwoods and ignore the cops and stuff. Most of the guys going in don't have a clue, so you talk with your cars, you figure out what to do. It's not hard.

As noted earlier, the term "cars" meant a fellow gang member; men also used the terms "homies" or "boys." Some of the skinhead gangs (i.e., PENI, the Peckerwoods, Aryan Brotherhood) are rivals. For example, the Nazi Low-Riders (NLR) and Public Enemy Number One gangs are rival gangs, but the PENI gangs have a history of working with the Aryan Brotherhood (also called the AB or Brand). Interviewees explained that the Aryan Brotherhood gang used to run with the Nazi Low-Riders. However, the NLR allowed some biracial men (Hispanic and white) to join their gang, and the Aryan Brotherhood did not like that decision.

It is easy to see why it is so important to socialize new inmates quickly. Men had to know friend from enemy, or they would get hurt. They relied on each other to help them acclimate to this social system. Luis spoke of this socialization to a family: "I met a lot of guys in prison who are like family to me. There are a lot of good people in prison who will help you out and show you how to be a man. Sure, I know a lot of guys that did more for me than my parents ever did. They showed me things and taught me things that I'll use for the rest of my life. My own parents didn't do that stuff for me." Tyler, a member of the Nazi Low-Rider skinhead gang, described how this process made him proud to be white:

> I went to prison early. I was nineteen when I first went in. I feel like I was raised in prison. The first time, that's when I got inked. I met my brothers in prison, and that was when I learned about the fight of the white man. The NLR guys, they raised me in prison, and they showed me how to fight for the white man. I learned to respect white women and to fight for my brothers inside. You have to learn that quickly; otherwise, you are nothing but a prison punk. I thank God everyday that I hooked up with the NLR.

Experienced inmates helped new ones learn the ropes in prison and how to survive. Those who were not following the prescribed prison norms were often targeted for violence. Racial segregation guided new inmates to people who would teach them the rules. Thus, gang members had an easy way to recruit.

What was especially interesting to me was how they posited the inmate as controlling the prison environment. To be sure, inmates are controlled by formal, prison rules, and correctional officers patrol every square foot of prison. However, men went to other inmates to learn how to behave. Through this process, they learned how to resolve conflict. They also learned who to associate with and when to fight. To a large extent, those rules shaped their prison identity, especially as it related to gang activity. According to Kevin D. Vryan, Patricia A. Adler, and Peter Adler,

> our identity is the part of our "self" that is public. It indicates a specific location within some form of social structure, whether that structure is seen as situational and transient or as an enduring effect of socially structured relations. Identity is also the aspect of the self that is most public, as it is perceived and interpreted during interaction with others. (Vryan, Adler, and Adler 2003:368)

Throughout the socialization process, inmates internalized the norms of their environment. Several men also described how their identity was shaped by gang membership. Fellow gang members showed men how to act like a prisoner and a gang member. Tyler explained how his work with the Nazi Low-Riders cemented his white identity and instructed him about the "fight of the white man."

Male prison inmates created a worthy identity through this interactive process if they acclimated to the informal rules of prison. The longer they stayed in prison, the easier the process became. Their daily interactions shaped cultural norms as gangs and violent action became an accepted part of prison life. Remember, the men I interviewed do not describe random acts of violence or chaos. Instead, they discussed a negotiation of violence.

Elijah Anderson (2000) discusses the importance of inner-city mentors, or "old heads," who teach young people, especially young men, how to behave. However, the problem is that many of these older men (usually men in their mid to late thirties) moved away from the inner cities since the 1980s, leaving young men to their own devices and giving them fewer "decent" mentors to show them the ropes. The men in my study also described mentors who showed young people entering prison how to act and how to acclimate to prison culture. However, these men taught newcomers when and where to fight and how to keep correctional officers out of the loop. At first blush, it seemed that those mentors were teaching young men how to be violent. However, unlike the men in Anderson's (2000) study, the men in prison were mentoring others in a total institution filled with convicted felons. Instead of the code of the street in the inner city, the men in prison learned the inmate code that, in part, told them how to survive in prison.

Those interviewed told me that men who broke rules brought unwanted attention to themselves and others. Therefore, mentors were tasked with teaching them when and where to fight. They taught them when to ignore racist epithets and when to attack someone in a prison blind spot, which is a low-surveillance area. In other words, they helped young men to assimilate and survive. New inmates, in turn, relied on gang leaders or older inmates to learn the established prison norms, which, to be sure, did little to break up gangs or stop violence altogether.

I do not contend that those mentors were teaching healthy or functional real world skills. In fact, the skinhead gangs who promote the white power ideology are especially troubling. However, the recent mass incarceration trend caused many problems in prison, including overcrowding, violence, and the rise of prison gangs (Hunt et al. 1993). According to the California Department of Corrections and Rehabilitation, their thirty-three facilities are working, on average, at 195 percent of capacity (California Department of Corrections and Rehabilitation 2010). Almost all their facilities are overcrowded, which could affect how inmates and correctional officers live and work together. By organizing their lives and controlling others, gang leaders maintained some semblance of autonomy and control. They lived under complete supervision, but informal norms allowed them to hold on to a little power and control some parts of their lives. Therefore, these norms and the men who mentor others were described as especially meaningful and important.

Mentoring and Mothering in Women's Prisons

Those studying incarcerated women find that they often create prison families (Foster 1975; Giallombardo 1974; Owen 1998). It is estimated that upward of 70 percent of incarcerated women create these families (MacKenzie, Robinson, and Campbell 1989; Propper 1982). Researchers also examine the lesbian relationships women have in prison (Bowker 1977; Clark 1995; Forsyth, Evans, and Foster 2002; Hampton 1993; Leger 1987; Propper 1982). Barbara Owen (1998) estimates 30 percent to 60 percent of incarcerated women engage in lesbian relationships. Some of these women identified as lesbians before entering prison, but most had same-sex relationships only while incarcerated. In general, they suffered from being separated from their families, particularly their children. Therefore, they formed deep emotional bonds with fellow inmates.

Much like the men I interviewed, the women stated that they mentored each other in prison. They often described their relationships as a family. At the same time, some of the women explained that they had to control one another because they did not want others to get into trouble. They also claimed that women are much easier to control than men. Again, they compared their experiences to those of men. Several women resented being treated like men. For example, Stella stated:

> Women in prison act much different than men in prison. We were treated like men, which I think is wrong. We don't act anything like men, and the guards treat us like dirt. They would yell at us and threaten us. All you have to do is ask or give us some direction; we'll follow whatever directions you give us and we won't fight back. Instead, they treat us like dogs, like men. It's overkill because we cooperate and follow the rules.

That was a common theme. They were not violent; therefore, correctional officers could take a gentle approach with them. Historically, the prison system was a masculine institution. Of course, women have always gone to prison, but men were always incarcerated at a higher rate. Also, men committed more violent offenses and were more likely to hurt each other in prison. Within my sample, 30 percent of the women were convicted for a violent offense (robbery, attempted murder, assault, domestic violence), whereas 83 percent of the men I interviewed were convicted of at least one violent offense (robbery, rape, assault, manslaughter, kidnapping).

Like other women I interviewed, Edith believed that they were put into a system that was never meant for them. "It's humiliating; they stick us in men's prisons, strip-search us like men, and talk to us like we are violent criminals. All the women I was in with were busted for drugs, no violence. We don't rape kids, and we don't beat our wives. If we were a bunch of murderers, I could see why they would act so rough, but what the hell?" Rita explained that women in prison are often damaged:

> Women grow up abused, girls who are abused, end up having sex a lot; they use drugs. Boys who get beaten end up beating up others. We get into drugs and shit: we hook up with men who get us using, then bam, we get busted. Men run wild, rape, and beat up their girlfriends and stuff. Now you explain to me why we all get treated the same? The men did all the real damage, and we just damaged ourselves; then we go to prison where we get slammed around by the guards. They need to have a different place for women.

Rita was convicted of a violent offense, robbery. However, she explains how her relationship with men led her to make bad decisions:

> When I was arrested, I had a lot of drugs on me, mostly weed and crank. I was arrested with my boyfriend. He used to deal and a guy owed him money, and he and I went to his place and beat him up pretty bad. A neighbor called the police, and they arrested us for breaking and entering, robbery and drug possession. I was on parole, so I got some serious time. Would I have been there without my man? No, ma'am. Do I take responsibility for my actions? Yes, I do. I did those things, and I will have to answer to God for them. But the good Lord knows that I would be a different person if I never met him. Our love of men takes us to some dark places.

Female inmates also described the stigma associated with incarceration. Molly discussed how prison altered her reputation:

> Do you know how people act when they find out you were in prison? They act shocked, probably because I'm a woman. People don't want you around their kids. You can't get jobs because you have to disclose your status. People I knew my whole life ignore me and won't speak to me. My own sister thinks I'm trash. I know guys who go to prison and get street cred; that is crazy. My life is completely changed now and not for the better, let me tell you.

Women who commit violent offenses were often described as pitiful rather than intimidating or frightening. Polly described how inmates reacted to women who kill their own children.

> POLLY: I knew some seriously messed-up women in prison. They hurt their children, or they shot their husbands and stuff. I knew this woman who killed her own kid.
>
> TRAMMELL: What was she like?
>
> POLLY: Sad, really sad. I mean, she killed her kid, so she's going to Hell. But this was a sad and sick woman. I almost felt sorry for her; she cried all the time and talked about her son. Sweet Jesus, it depressed me, so I avoided her.

Bella talked about women who suffer from mental illness:

> I knew some women who scared me, that's for sure. The women who were just crazy, you know? You don't know if they are going to smile at you or punch you out. I had a cellie once who used to throw herself around the cell, screaming her head off. You can't do anything with that! You know who the crazy women are; they are the screamers and such. They probably did drugs all of their lives and now they're just screwed up.

Women feared uncontrollable inmates but often created a backstory about their situation, generally one in which the women were victims. Their crimes may or may not have affected their prison identity, but their prison identity certainly influenced what fellow inmates thought of them. Their sympathy for other inmates often drove them to reach out to help young or vulnerable women. This helped them maintain a positive public identity as a mentor or caregiver. They described these relationships as family units, with a mom and a dad; the father figure often disciplined the "kids" that they took under their wing. Emily told me what it meant to be the dad in a prison family.

> EMILY: They called me "dad" in prison cuz I was like a father figure for these girls. Lots of girls do not know how to show respect because they grew up in the system and now they're fucked up. I had to sit them down and say, "Knock that shit off"; they'd listen to me and learn to clean up their act.
>
> TRAMMELL: And if they don't?
>
> EMILY: They did, or I had to set them straight. I knocked this girl around once; she was one of my kids, and she kept saying shit to the guards. She would tie up her shirt so her stomach showed and she carried on. You see they have no manners. You have to get serious with

them right away or they bring a lot of shit onto themselves. They learn the right way, or they end up in trouble. I'm doing them a favor.

Hannah had to stop mentoring one of her kids because she was selling drugs: "I tried to help this one girl, take her in, teach her how to act. She ended up smuggling in drugs, which is a serious offense. I had to cut her loose. I'm not working with girls who just want to do hard time and end up serving longer cuz they are committing felonies in prison. I'll work with the kids who want help."

Helping young girls in prison was important, according to Rosa:

> You don't understand. Young women go to prison now, eighteen or nineteen years old. These are girls we're talking about. They have no idea how to act in prison, and no one told them how to behave or how to stay out of trouble. I knew of so many street girls in prison; they'd been on the street for years before they went in. I figure it was my duty to help them. I have daughters, and I would hope that someone would take care of my little ones if they ever went away.

Sofia discussed how she and her prison girlfriend helped mentor a troubled young woman: "My girl and I took care of this girl who got in a lot of trouble, at first. Once we worked with her, she did fine. I think that a lot of women in prison were never disciplined. That's probably why some of them are in prison. No dad, mom works too many jobs or is hooked on drugs or something; this means that they raise themselves."

Like some of the men I interviewed, Alexandria stressed how important it was to learn to follow the rules.

> ALEXANDRIA: If you know what to do, it's easier. The problem is that there are too many young women coming into prison. They come in, like eighteen or nineteen years old, and a lot of them went through CYA [California Youth Authority]; now they grew up in the system. They don't have any manners, and they don't know how to behave. That's going to get you hurt. I knew of a girl who had no table manners; she would grab stuff off of other girls' plate. You don't do that stuff! Other girls, they think they know everything; you can't tell them anything. It's always the young girls. I really feel sorry for them; I can't imagine growing up in this system. What the hell is going to happen to them when they finally get out of prison?
>
> TRAMMELL: How did you deal with these women?
>
> ALEXANDRIA: You do everything you can to teach them, work with them. I tried not to give up on these girls, but I have to wonder about

their parents. Where are their parents? Why did they fail these girls? That's what I want to know.

To Ella, watching out for others is simply what women do:

Women take care of each other, plain and simple. You see women in prison making families, making their cell nice and homey. They get girlfriends and hold hands. They need someone to talk to, you know, someone to listen to them. The new girls would come in and you could hear them crying at night, and it broke my heart. I would try to reach out to them, get them to talk. You would have to show them the ropes, you know where everything is, who to avoid, which officer is going to be nice to you and help you out.

Women in prison are forced to help each other because no one else will. As Charlotte explained, there are few services for women.

Who is going to help us in prison? No one, that's who. We would get with the new girls, show them the ropes, and we'd meet with the girls who were leaving. We'd ask them: Do you have a plan? Do you have some place to stay? How are you going to get a job? Stuff like that. I talked to this one girl; she said that she was going to go to Ramon's place, and I know that's her pimp. I gave her the name of my sister; she contacted her, and [my sister] drove the girl around putting in her application. She let her stay on her couch for a while. The girl did not go back to her pimp. I think I may have saved that girl's life. What did the state of California do for her? Nothing!

These families served several purposes. First, they helped women cope with the pain of incarceration. Second, these "family" structures encouraged women to mentor each other in prison. It was better for everyone to avoid trouble, so the more experienced inmates adopted some "kids" and took them under their wings. They also promoted the norm of civility. They believed that young girls who entered prison were in dire need of mentoring and mothering. Unlike men, they described their behavior as caregiving. They explained that prison was very hard on women, and they felt sorry for young girls who were lost. Unlike the men, who enforced rules partly to keep the prison staff at a distance, these women believed that they were saving these women from themselves. They taught them life lessons and made sure they had a place to go after they parole. Of course, making families also meant that they must discipline these girls to "set them straight." They had a moral obligation to help women.

By comparing the stories of men and women, we see clear examples about how inmates adhere to their prescribed gender roles. Lori B. Girshick (2000:19–20) stated: "Gender roles are expectations that define acceptable behaviors and attitudes for children and adults of both sexes; deviation may result in a variety of sanctions, ranging from ostracism to name calling to violence to incarceration." She argued that women who depart from traditional gender roles are labeled "deviant." The stories told by these women detail how women were taught not to misbehave.

One difference between the male and female inmates is that the women tried to make fellow inmates better people. Men, however, simply wanted to control their environment. They may also have wanted to maintain their businesses or to keep the staff at bay. Conversely, women generally wanted to force women to behave in a civilized manner, that is, adhere to traditional gender roles. Acting out was unacceptable, so women were "taught" how to behave properly. This is mostly done in a social context that resembled the nuclear family. The woman occupying the role of the father is charged with disciplining the unruly children.

Young women took the place of older inmates' own children, so they got to take on the role of nurturer while incarcerated. They believed that no one else was willing to help these women. They blamed parents, the prison system, and the state of California for failing them. They felt that women, as criminals, were not has harmful as men and should be taken care of in a different manner. Simply put, prison, and the indignity that goes with incarceration, should be reserved for those who do real harm.

The focus on caring for other inmates and the belief that the system victimizes women were quite different from the stories told by the men in my study. They explained how they controlled each other and their environment. Men did not talk about nurturing each other or how they were concerned about fellow inmates. At first blush, we could explain these differences according to traditional gender roles. It seems clear, however, that both men and women believed that mentoring others served a greater purpose. It taught new inmates the norms of prison, allowing them to maintain their culture and their sense of empowerment. At the end of the day, no one wanted chaos.

It has long been argued that our friends and family members serve as a mechanism for social control (Berger 1963). Inmates form families in prison in order to gain some control of prison society. These men and women claimed their main problems were with correctional officers and problem inmates and expressed their desire to keep such people at a distance. To accomplish those goals, they had to reach out to new inmates to help them assimilate. Their solution was to band together to survive the difficulties of prison.

As others have shown, women usually seek out interpersonal connections; relationships are quite important (Chodorow 1978; Gilligan 1982). Because of gender socialization, girls and women learn how to make connections and maintain friendships throughout their lives. They take care of each other, which influences the prison environment and culture. They described an environment in which the inmates created families and networks in order to protect each other. Conversely, the men described a type of hypermasculine hierarchy in which the leaders call the shots and show them the ropes. Both men and women did these things to avoid conflict with the prison staff. However, women discussed the importance of following the rules, whereas men tried to take charge of their environment. Inmates lose their freedom and their ability to make simple, daily decisions. In order to gain back some of this freedom, they make every attempt to control their environment by developing informal norms about conflict resolution.

Conclusion

In this chapter, I outlined some of the ways in which inmates developed and maintained informal norms in prison. The creation of these norms raises two questions. First, why do they maintain this particular social structure in prison? One logical answer is that inmates describe this system as adversarial in nature. Both men and some women have problems with correctional officers. They also suffer the pains of incarceration, such as the fear of violence and the loss of freedom. Therefore, there is strength in numbers. They seek out social groups (gangs, cliques, prison families) who help them assimilate. Moreover, these groups reinforce the "us versus them" culture of prison, which creates a standard in-group/out-group dynamic. Inmates create social groups and then describe the out-group as inferior. The men, for example, described incompetent and lazy correctional officers who are easily duped. Some women complained that correctional officers treat them too roughly. Also, they talked about the system being against them. Simply put, men described being smarter than their out-group, and women described being a victim of the system. Either case hardly makes for a rehabilitative environment.

Prisons, like all formal punishment, supposedly function to deter, rehabilitate, and incapacitate the inmate as well as provide retribution for crime victims (Bedau 1987). However, inmates' descriptions of prison centered on how they created a united front against this institution. They could not effectively or openly rebel against the prison, so they carefully worked around the system to maintain a semblance of power. The so-called inmate code does not allow inmates to work directly with prison staff (Hassine 2007; Sykes 1958; Terry 1997; Trammell 2009b). Officially, correctional officers are not allowed to form personal relationships with the inmates or become entangled in the inmate subculture (California Department of Corrections and Rehabilitation 2003). Although those rules are good ones that reduce the chance of corruption or abuse, together the formal and informal rules help solidify in-group dynamics. As Sampson and Bean (2006:28) pointed out: "The hard facts of social structure—the economy, the state, violence—are themselves continually produced and enacted by our skillful and purposive social action. Culture plays a structural role in the making of this world." Our understanding of our culture comes from interacting with others. This, in turn, creates our social reality and worldview. The formal structure of prison, in conjunction with the daily interaction between inmates and correctional officers, shapes prison culture.

Interviewees explained, for example, how they had to be taught how to act in prison. They had to be shown which friends were appropriate, how to manipulate correctional officers, and how to avoid problems. They saw prison as an adversarial system in which you had to distinguish friend from foe very quickly. Mentoring new inmates provided the perfect opportunity to socialize them. This is not to say that their personal values were checked at the prison gate. However, it seemed clear that they created and managed another culture inside prison centered on the very notion of surviving prison.

What every citizen and taxpayer should be asking is, how does this promote rehabilitation? California has one of the highest recidivism rates in the nation (70 percent), and over half return to prison on technical (parole) violations (Fischer 2005). In other words, they "broke parole" by using drugs or alcohol, associated with another felon, failed to report to their parole officer, and/or violated other conditions of parole. Whether they went back to jail on a technical violation or reoffended, what, exactly, does prison teach the inmate? That is not an easy question to answer.

Most of the people in my study occupied their time by maintaining a subculture while focusing on underground economies and survival. Furthermore, they described how they sold drugs, joined gangs, and protected each other from those who were tasked with helping them rehabilitate. Although it is not possible, using the data from this book, to determine the extent to which interviewees were rehabilitated, it seems clear that their stint in prison was not entirely productive. Moreover, these interviews detail the problem of modern American corrections from the perspective of the inmate. As pointed out in *Confronting Confinement: A Report of the Commission on Safety and Abuse in America's Prisons* (Gibbons and Katzenbach 2006:6):

> For all of the hard work and achievements of corrections professionals—most of which the public does not hear about—there is still too much violence in America's prisons and jails, too many facilities that are crowded to the breaking point, too little medical and mental health care, unnecessary uses of solitary confinement and other forms of segregation, a desperate need for the kinds of productive activities that discourage violence and make rehabilitation possible, and a culture in many prisons and jails that pits staff against prisoners and management against staff.

From the perspective of the inmate, they are challenged from day one to survive in a facility where there is little trust between themselves and prison staff. They mentor each other because they want to control their environment. They want new inmates to behave in accordance with established norms. However, this means that inmates are resocialized by their prison experience. Over 90 percent of inmates leave prison and return to their communities (Petersilia 2003). They step into prisons a convicted felon. It seems reasonable to be concerned about what they are when they leave.

A second question raised by inmates' creation of prison norms is, what happens when solidarity breaks down and conflict occurs between inmates rather than between staff and inmates? In the remaining chapters, I focus on violence and interpersonal conflict between inmates. In doing so, I discuss issues such as race, gender, and social control. One thing to keep in mind is that there is evidence that inmates refuse to report a good deal of violence. They prefer to deal with daily problems outside the confines of institutional sanctions.

3

Race and Gangs

Since the 1970s, African Americans and Hispanics have entered prison at an alarming rate in the United States. In 1960, approximately 65 percent of inmates were white (Tonry 1995); however, as of December 2005, African Americans and Hispanics represented 60 percent of state and federal inmates (Harrison and Beck 2006). At the time of my data collection, approximately 67 percent of male inmates in California were African American or Hispanic (California Department of Corrections and Rehabilitation 2010).

Many blame the war on drugs for this trend (Parenti 1999; Reiman 2001; Sterling 1998; Tonry 1995; Wacquant 2001). For example, Michael Tonry (1995) pointed out that by the end of the 1980s, minorities were arrested on drug charges at a rate five times higher than white offenders. Others find that minorities are more likely to be arrested, convicted, and given longer sentences than white defendants (Henderson, Cullen, and Carrol 2000; Parker, Dewees, and Radelet 2001; Wacquant 2001). Furthermore, young African American men are more likely to be charged with a violent crime or be the victim of violence than members of any other group (Renzetti 2006).

In some states, such as California and Texas, male inmates segregated along racial lines and joined prison gangs (Jacobs 1977; Orlando-Morningstar 1997; Parenti 1999; Wacquant 2001). However, officials in Texas successfully desegregated their state prisons by enforcing random cell assignment in an incremental manner (Trulson and Marquart 2009). They also had a designated space for problem inmates during the era of desegregation.

Of course, this begs the question, why do some men segregate by race in prison? To a large degree, we can blame the changes in prison culture effected by the large number of people, especially minorities, entering prison. In other words, as prisons filled beyond capacity, prison norms changed. Cognitive psychologists find that we identify each other through a cognitive process in which we recognize and attenuate toward race and gender cues (Davidenko 2007). When we first meet someone, we identify that person's gender and race almost immediately. In a same-sex environment such as prison, race becomes an easy way to divide and create in-group alliances. As we create alliances, we come to identify strongly with our in-group and distrust, or even despise, people in the out-group (Tajfel and Turner 1979; Vaghan, Tajfel, and Williams 1981). This tendency could explain some of the initial racial divisions that occur in some prisons. To explore the reasons why men promote and support ongoing racial segregation, we should look at how inmates explain their cultural norms about this issue. First, let's examine the history of racial segregation in California prisons.

Segregation was always the norm in California prisons. Of course, prison officials did little to address this problem until very recently. As Chad R. Trulson and James W. Marquart (2009:213) point out: "By 2005, no official policy existed with regard to racial segregation in housing. Rather, racial segregation was a longtime practice that had existed since the beginnings of that prison system. . . . According to California prison officials, racially segregated double cells prevented violence among rival gang members aligned along racial and ethnic lines." The authors describe the California system as "ground zero" for racially identified prison gangs in the United States.

In the early years of mass incarceration, John Irwin (1980) found that men in California prisons in the 1970s segregated into intraracial groups, and some men formed white power gangs. For example, skinhead gangs such as the Nazi Low-Riders and Public Enemy Number One originated in California prisons (Anti-Defamation League 2005; Southern Poverty Law Center 2001). Geoffrey Hunt and his colleagues (1993) found that men in prison used race as a way to create gangs or cliques. When the prison population was small, men identified homies as men from their neighborhoods or cities, that is, men from back home.

As the population grew, homies were identified as men of the same race. In this sense, prisons were Balkanized as the population grew and race became an easy way to create in-group alliances. The fact that in 2008 African American men represented 29 percent of inmates and Hispanic men represent 38 percent made race especially relevant to white men in California prisons (California Department of Corrections and Rehabilitation 2008a).

Philip Goodman (2008) conducted an ethnography of prison reception centers and found that California correctional officers forced inmates to "choose/state" their race and then to state whether or not they could share a cell with someone of a different race. If they answered "yes," they were asked again until the inmate figured out that the correct answer was no. This process undoubtedly helped male inmates organize their social networks by race (Goodman 2008). More important, this practice by officers institutionalized racial segregation for the sake of keeping the peace and reducing violence. Historically, prison administrators in California locked prisons down by race if violence occurred. However, in the *Johnson v. California et al.* (2005) Supreme Court decision, the Court determined that racial segregation in prison is unconstitutional. Thus, prison officials in California cannot officially separate inmates by race. However, if inmates specifically request to be in a cell with people of their own race, the correctional officer obliges. Hence, the "state your race and whether or not you can share a cell with someone of another race" strategy works to segregate the cells (Goodman 2008) and probably reduces violence. As pointed out by Trulson and Marquart (2009), prison employees separated inmates by race to keep rival gangs from hurting each other.

Outside prison, whites make up approximately 72.4 percent of the US population (Humes, Jones, and Ramirez 2011) but only 27 percent of the population in men's prisons in California (California Department of Corrections and Rehabilitation 2008a). Undoubtedly, many people find white power groups offensive. However, their presence clearly shows that some white men responded to a shift in racial demographics by maintaining a strong racial identity. This is a rational, albeit disturbing, choice for men who probably never had to think about race from the perspective of a minority population.

In comparison, state officials in Texas desegregated their system and now enjoy the most racially integrated system in the United States. It is important to note that they did not encounter a high level of violence in doing so. It is possible to desegregate prisons, although Trulson and Marquart (2009:215) pointed out that there is no one-size-fits-all approach to accomplishing this task:

> We do not offer sweeping claims as to whether desegregation can be realized in other prison systems and whether the lessons learned from Texas can apply equally outside its borders. No two prisons systems are alike; population, racial composition, physical capacity, existing infrastructure, experience with institutional litigation, legislative support, political climate, regional variations, relationships between inmates

and staff, states' racial history, and budgets are only a few of the innumerable ways prison systems may differ, and there are dozens more that might preclude applying the Texas experience elsewhere.

The Norms of Segregation

All the men in my study told me that that it was impossible to desegregate men's prisons in California. However, many had friends or associates of other races in prison, and they claimed to sell drugs or other illegal items to anyone who could pay. In other words, they wanted residential segregation but were flexible when it came to business or friendship. They stated that gang leaders ("leaders" or "shot-callers") had to control norms about race relations. These leaders often worked with gang members to resolve conflict. Make no mistake, these men ran underground businesses and were responsible for causing violence. However, the men stated that shot-callers prevented violence as well. They told me that fights were most likely to happen over drug debts, race, and disrespect. To avoid formal sanctions, leaders had to stay on top of those particular issues, and other inmates had to avoid problems with prison staff.

As Trulson and Marquart (2009) state, one factor affecting segregation is the relationship between inmates and staff. In the previous chapter, I outlined how inmates distanced themselves from staff, especially correctional officers. They trained new inmates to rely on fellow inmates for help and guidance. Miguel discussed his relationship with correctional officers:

> You need to make your own way and do good time. The cops will pretend to help you to get information, but they are not your friends. You get the new guys coming in; they want to make all kinds of changes and they will run around and really hustle. The old guys, the ones who worked in prisons for a long time, they know the deal and they just leave you alone and do shit at work. The guys in the middle, those fuckers are more likely to slam you around. They absolutely cannot be trusted, and they will plot to make trouble. I can stand the young and the old guys but not those guys who have worked two or three years.

Carlos told me this story about hazing officers who are new on the job:

> We would fuck with the new cops. If they were young they'd be scared and we would stare them down. You know, the other COs would fuck with them too. I knew this guy who maybe had one week under his belt and the other guys convinced him that one of my boys was a se-

rious mass murderer or something. Then they made sure that he transported him and locked him between the doors for like, five minutes. The new guy is pissing his pants, sweating and stuff and kept saying that he's claustrophobic. My boy just gave him a smile which made him really nervous. No harm, right? We've all been the new guy and gone through that shit, right?

One of Rey's friends hit a correctional officer. When that happens, the correctional officers get a few "free shots" at the inmate: they cuff them and then punch them a few times.

> They can make things rough. The guy who hit the cop, he learned to keep his hands to himself. They cuffed him and took a few turns knocking him around. He was bleeding from his nose pretty bad and they left him bleeding in his cell, handcuffed behind his back. Just lying there, bleeding. You don't fuck with those guys, man. The older guys, they're okay. They want to run out their days and they'll actually be cool to us and I've seen them roll their eyes at the young guys who don't know shit.

These men detail an interesting relationship between correctional officers and inmates. There is some animosity between these groups, but inmates encourage each other to learn who they can work with and who to avoid. Seth told me that correctional officers knew a lot about the gangs:

> When I went in, the officers told me that it didn't matter who I ran with. I'm white, so I know I'll hang with the white guys, but the officers said that they didn't care. But you know what? They knew more about the gangs and shit than I thought they would. They knew who was in what gang and if there was going to be problems. I know people snitch and stuff, so I guess that's it. They knew that I hated the Peckerwoods, and they would say things about playing nice with the woods and stuff.

Technically, being in a gang in California prisons is a punishable offense. One way to deal with gangs is to split them up and send the leaders to administrative segregation units. Also, prison administrators sometimes transfer gang members to other prisons. Inmates can, and do, lose their good-time credit and face formal sanctions if they participate in gang-related activity. Clearly, prison officials have formal options when dealing with prison gangs.

Prison officials may also participate in some forms of informal negotiation as well. Christian Parenti (1999) argued that it was advantageous for the correctional officers to allow gang leaders to control inmates. Therefore, there is no real effort to eliminate gangs. Instead, correctional officers work to direct and manage violence away from prison staff (Parenti 1999). Of course, this means that they want the gangs to fight each other. However, my interviewees described a negotiated order (Fine 1984; Maines 1982; Maines and Charlton 1985; Nathan and Mitroff 1991; Scott 2009). As inmates and correctional officers interacted with one another, they learned to avoid conflict. Miguel and Rey explained that the longer men serve as correctional officers, the more likely they are to avoid conflict. Rey gave an example of this "negotiation" in which correctional officers informally punished those who attacked them. Also, inmates are told that it does not matter who they run with, but then officers gather as much information as possible about the gangs. To reduce conflict, each side gathers information on the other group.

Finally, the men in my study described how gangs self-regulate to avoid riots or other forms of violence. In other words, prison became an organization in which informal rules worked along with formal mandates to reduce conflict and maintain order. Each prison gang is organized vertically; leadership is highly important. But there is also a horizontal organization between gangs and prison staff, which helps coordinate the lives of the inmates. To be sure, there is violence in these facilities. However, it seems clear that no one wants chaos.

The Role of the Gang Leader

Former inmates explained that gangs control drugs, prostitution, pornography, and most recently, the cigarette trade in prison. Leaders, or shot-callers, rise through the ranks and prove their loyalty to the gangs; men called this "putting in your time." Luis defined a shot-caller this way:

> A shot-caller is someone that runs the whole tank or module. Pretty much, people that know a lot about incarceration cuz they've been in prison for a while. They run it and they run the section; they talk about what's going on. That environment, it's negative; it's politics. If an argument breaks out, the shot-caller will go over there and say, "What's the situation that happened with the race and stuff?" They then talk and see if they can solve it. If they can't solve it then they say, "You know what man? You better do something. That guy that started something, he better get out of the module," or they fight.

Roman explains how the older inmates have more experience and are more likely to help reduce conflict:

So here's the deal, you got old guys like me who have been in prison forever and have shot-callers do their job, keep peace and run the action. That's why we have shot-callers so when a couple of idiots get into it in the yard, instead of letting them kill themselves, the shot-caller goes out and works it out. He talks to these guys and finds out what happened, who did what to who, it's very simple. If we didn't have these guys, the businesses would stop. These guys are very important.

Luis and Roman would go to their leaders for advice on when and where to fight. These leaders were not necessarily peacekeepers. Instead, they served to control and contain the violence in order to avoid institutional sanctions such as a lockdown.

Of course, there were norms about racial segregation. Luke explained that inmates will fight desegregation efforts: "They can't tell us who to cell with. I know the cops and stuff, they want us to cell up with the blacks and Mexicans, but they will never ever get away with that. We'll take control of the prison. Look, they can lock me up and they can force us in the hole, but it isn't going to work; they'll never get the guys in prison to cell up, won't happen." Tyler, a shot-caller in prison, told me how he controlled race relations in prison:

We have to keep control on the race thing. I was fine with the boys playing cards or dealing meth to the blacks and the Southerners and stuff, that's fine. Celling-up is another story. If I don't check my boys, then I look weak to the other leaders. This is like a power play. It's complicated. We are the minority in prison; we are, um, the whites are under the thumb of the other guys, especially the Southerners, so we have to have a united front and play it tough. I have to let the other guys know that we don't roll that way; we stick with our own. Now what does that mean? It's a lot about appearances; I really don't give a shit about your friends. I had a guy that played serious poker and won lots of money from the black guys in prison; that was great, keep up the good work, my brother. But if he told me he was going to the blacks to cell up, then I check him. I gotta get my boys to put him in check. He represents me and my boys, so he better recognize.

The Negotiation of Race Relations in Men's Prisons

Several men use the term "political" to describe prison norms. For example, Adam stated:

It's very political and well, there's a part in the Bible that says that the races should not mix. That's why we're separated in the first place, and so inside there, when you're incarcerated, it's the same thing. You're not to mix races, you're not to sit next to someone of a different race other than your own race, eat with someone other than of your own race, smoke with someone other than of your race. Someone has to control this, and so our leader regulates these things.

They used this term to explain how their social organization was routinized and structured by the powers that be. It was political because leaders often worked together to create rules that inmates had to follow.

Although Adam said there was no contact between men of different races, the majority of the men I interviewed (75 percent) told me they had interracial relationships in prison. They played cards, socialized, and dealt drugs with their friends or associates of different races. At the same time, sharing a cell with someone of another race was strictly forbidden. Martino described having friends of different races: "No, we talk to whoever. You're right that we don't stick by people of other races. If a fight breaks out, I'm not going to defend a white guy or something, but I'll talk to one in the yard. Play cards or something. I've played cards with people that I'm fighting with half an hour later. Then we go back to playing cards." Evan explained how racism developed in this atmosphere:

> If you go to the yard, you see the whites together and the blacks together and the Mexicans together, and we all eat with our own kind, but it's hard to describe. I did talk with blacks and stuff, it's not like, "Don't talk to me or I'll fight you." It's not like that. We fight about race and there is a lot of racism; I'm not going to lie to you. People in there hate each other. I just don't know if they really hate each other or they just hate that place. I don't hate blacks now that I'm out, but I sure avoided them in prison. I think that the guys inside are just angry and need to push that hate onto someone.

Brad told a story about a fight he witnessed and how it would only hurt the instigator in the end:

> I saw this fight go down . . . a white guy jumped a black guy and yelled "white power." The guy wasn't in a gang yet; he was a new guy. I know that they make them do that shit to join the gangs, and I know that this guy is now going to the hole and then he'll be a target for the blacks. I know that. It still pisses me off, as a black man. When you're inside, you just pissed, all the time. You're pissed at each other and you're pissed because you don't get visitors. You're pissed because you're scared, and the gangs feed on this. This "divide the yard" shit makes it easy to see who to hate. I just don't know if the boys see it that way. They get into this stuff and don't realize that they only hurt themselves.

Both Brad and Evan described the frustration of being an inmate. They blamed racism in California prisons on the fact that inmates were very angry people. Are these men truly racist? That is hard to determine. However, it seems clear that they must appear to support segregation and racist norms. Brad went so far as to suggest that racism actually hurt these men in the long run. This is a cyclical problem in which men become angry about incarceration and direct that anger at others, and these public displays make men on both sides of the dispute even angrier.

James, however, described race relations as flexible as long as you followed the rules:

> The races don't officially mix. That's true, but you can buy drugs from whoever, and the leaders control that stuff. I've had a cigarette with some white guys, and the Mexicans, the Southerners, are mostly good guys. Their leaders are, well, some of them are flexible with their boys. It's not as cut and dried as you think. But if a fight breaks out, then yes, the races stick together. If the blacks and whites go at it, I'm in and I'm taking down some white guys.

It is interesting he said that "the races don't officially mix" because, officially, California was supposed to integrate its prisons. He talked about informal norms about segregation as if they were formal mandates. It seems these men remain loyal to informal leaders rather than official rules. In fact, they refer to those norms as formal rules.

It appears that California prisons have developed three levels of social organization. First, there are the formal rules set up and enforced by the prison administration. Second, there is the norm of racial segregation, which has been in place for decades (Irwin 1980; Trulson and Marquart 2009). Third, there are daily interactions that are guided by both formal and informal rules. On the surface, the boys "don't mix." However, the presences of underground businesses, along with the flexibility of some of the leaders, allowed men to communicate and negotiate with men of all races. They went to great lengths to maintain the appearance of racial segregation and then continued having some friends of other races. Racism did not seem to be a chief motivation, but these norms guaranteed that segregation was coordinated. The fact that inmates fight for the men of their own race indicates that these racist displays are key to maintaining a positive public identity. Samuel explained how these rules increased the chance of violence:

> Oh, no, the races stick together. Go out in the yard; it's really amazing. The blacks are together; the whites are together; it's something. It's

more about fighting; if a fight breaks out, then you know who to hit [laughs]. You hit the guy that doesn't look like you. The weights and stuff, we marked them and stuff to keep our own stuff to us. We won't eat or sleep together, but I had white friends and stuff in prison. I mean, I could talk to whoever. It's complicated, it's very political, and the system works, but I have free will, I can hang out, talk with Mexican guys or something.

Men described fights as racial; if a fight broke out (over anything), the races divided. Should that happen, men defended their race by sticking together. A fight was a very public event; therefore, you had to show loyalty by sticking with your own race. To sell drugs, however, inmates had to be careful or they got caught. There were fewer public displays of this behavior. Samuel stated that he had "free will," which was not entirely true. Instead, the norms about race dictate that he can have friends of different races at the appropriate time. In this sense, informal norms shape the daily lives of men as they coordinate action. Roman told me this story:

> They asked me if I could cell up with a white guy; he was a PENI guy. I told them I couldn't, and they told me it was that or the hole. Okay, fine, put me in. I can't roll with the PENI guys. I know that the prison people, they have to try to get the boys to cell up together, but it will never happen; it'll be war. It's about your reputation . . . if I get to the yard and I'm celling up with the PENI guy, I'm facing some serious shit from my own guys. I didn't make the rules. I just follow them, and the guards, they can say what they want, but they don't make the rules; we do. Talk to the shot-callers; they'll tell you what's what.

Roman, who is Mexican, identified his proposed cellmate by his tattoos and knew he was a skinhead, which meant he couldn't share a cell with him. In other words, he didn't not fear a formal reprimand; he feared the retaliation from his own gang.

Of course, problems exist between gangs of the same race. Race is not the only reason men separate in prison. Max explained how men studied tattoos to determine gang affiliation and who was selling which drug:

> I ran with the PENI guys, mostly. I got all the right tattoos, and I only worked for them. We could tell who was NLR and who was AB by the tattoos and where they hung out. We would split up the yard and work. I didn't really care much about the politics; I just wanted to get it over with without going on someone's list. If you keep your head down

and stick with your boys, you'll do fine. It takes a few weeks, maybe
not that long, but you figure out pretty quick who's who and who runs
with who and who your boys are.

Once you learned whom to associate with, according to Max, you
had an easier time. Again, men tried to stay out of trouble. If they learned
the rules quickly, they did well in prison. Bobby, a member of the PENI
skinhead gang, told me this story: "I'm not listening to the cops. Screw
those guys. One guy tells me to clean up the TV room after some NLR
pricks are in there. I tell him that's not my job and I'm PENI so no way
I'm cleaning up after them. He threatens me with a 115 or worse and I
just laugh. What the hell is he going to do to me?" Max described "keeping his head down," whereas Bobby told me that he defied the orders of
a correctional officer. In either case, they remained loyal to "their own,"
which in these cases meant gang, not race. Furthermore, there are alliances between some Hispanic and white gangs and between some
African American and Hispanic gangs. It is a gross oversimplification to
assume that people simply go to prison and associate with people of their
own race until they are paroled.

As men enter prison, they are taught the basic rules of race relations.
If they learn the ropes early, they have few problems. If they have problems, leaders are there to negotiate and resolve conflict. This is not to
say that there are no problems or little violence, but it does seem clear that
these men worked hard to structure their own lives. In addition, they coordinated action in a way that reduced some conflict between the inmates
and correctional officers. In other words, correctional officers have to
break up fewer fights as inmates learn to solve their own problems. According to Goffman (1983:3):

> When in each other's presence, individuals are admirably placed to
> share a joint focus on attention, perceive that they do so, and perceive
> this perceiving. This, in conjunction with their capacity to indicate their
> own courses of physical action and to rapidly convey reactions to such
> indications from others provides the precondition for something cru-
> cial: the sustained, intimate coordination of action, whether in support
> of closely collaborative tasks or as a means of accommodating closely
> adjacent ones.

This idea is rooted in what Goffman calls the interaction order, which
takes place during face-to-face encounters (Goffman 1959, 1983). The
goal is to coordinate behavior to follow the path of least resistance. In jail,
segregation is coordinated in order to reduce conflict and maintain the
status quo. Of course, appearances matter, so men fight for their race and

refuse to cell up with a man of another race. Otherwise, their performance would be disingenuous, and they would have problems with their friends and gang members. This coordinated action around race causes problem for correctional officers; however, they must work around these rules in order to avoid violence.

It makes little sense to ask if these men are truly racist. Clearly, racist norms are embedded in the decision to segregate. However, it was not clear that all the men in my study were committed to a racist ideology. Instead, many were dedicated to maintaining a believable performance of racism. These men seemed to be very concerned about appearances, and they feared their own gang members more than they feared formal reprimands.

By controlling race relations, male inmates maintained some power over their environment. It is quite likely that some of these men truly believe that the races should never mix, but controlling interpersonal relationships makes it appear as if they had some control over their environment. On one hand, these men were inmates in a total institution. On the other hand, they controlled their environment by fighting for segregation. The Johnson Supreme Court decision (*Johnson v. California et al.* 2005) mandates desegregation in American prisons. Interviewees were upset about this decision because it challenged their social norms. They may or may not agree with racial segregation. In fact, most of them claim that they are not racist. The problem is the loss of control. They created all of these rules about roommates, and they worked with correctional staff to maintain these norms. They were offended that the Supreme Court could officially challenge these norms and tell them what to do. In this sense, this may have little to do with race.

Ideas to Promote Desegregation

In Texas, officials were very careful to classify and match inmates in a way that minimized violence. If California used Texas as a model, prison administrators would need a staff that is seriously dedicated to the desegregation of prison. A positive relationship between inmates and staff should facilitate the process (Trulson and Marquart 2009). From what these male inmates told me, they structured their behavior so as to distance themselves from prison staff. If the California Department of Corrections and Rehabilitation wants to desegregate, staff will need to remove some of these barriers and work with the inmates.

One obvious way to do this is to bring some of the inmate leaders into the discussion and work with them, but that is a problem for three reasons. First, there are rules against being in a gang. Gang leaders are often transferred and, in extreme cases, put in solitary confinement. Therefore, prison staff would need to relax the rules about gangs. Second, the inmates despise snitches and would not take kindly to their leaders openly working with prison staff. Third, there is no incentive for the men to desegregate.

If prison officials relaxed their policies about gangs and offered significant incentives, it might help them achieve their goal. As it stands now, prison officials have been ordered to release thousands of inmates (*Schwarzenegger v. Plata* 2010). Reducing the number of inmates should give them some room to work with and isolate inmates who are making trouble. I discuss this and other recommendations in more detail in the final chapter.

Race and Conflict in Women's Prisons

For women, the issue of race is also complicated. They do not segregate, and the women in my study told me that they generally follow the rules. When they were told to share a cell with a randomly assigned woman, they complied. Several women told me that they had no problem with their cellmates and that race is a "guy problem." For example, Julia explained that violence is rare in prison: "We had no problems; we got along. It's true that at the end of the day, women are better than men; we are more civilized; we are more caring. No one wants to see someone else get hurt. Men are different."

Joanne told me this story about an interracial friendship: "My best friend in prison is white. Her daughter died in a car accident, and we started talking, one day, about how we both lost our children. It united us, and we were always together. I did not care that she was white, and she did not care that I was black. I'm telling you right now, it does not matter. We were all in this together in prison." Many women offered similar stories about their prison friends. Both Julia and Joanne wanted friends to bond with; race did not matter to them. Many women in prison are mothers, and they bonded because of this shared status. The priorities of these women differed sharply from those of the men I interviewed. None of the men in my study discussed their children, and they described race as an easy way to divide.

At the same time, some women did fight in prison. Alexandria told me about the problems she had with her cellmate. She described the frustration of living with randomly assigned roommates.

> ALEXANDRIA: I have never met a meaner woman in my life. She was just plain mean. She would say shit to me all the time, trash our cell. It was a nightmare.
>
> TRAMMELL: Could you ask for another cellmate?
>
> ALEXANDRIA: Yes, I did, but no one cared. If I was a man I could just beat her up and they would give me a new cellie, but instead I took it. Nothing I could do.
>
> TRAMMELL: You mean that women don't get the same privileges [as] men because they are less violent?
>
> ALEXANDRIA: Here's the thing. Men riot, men rape each other, men beat the shit out of their cellie, and what happens? Maybe they get some time in the hole, but mostly, they get a new cellie, they get more yard time, they get whatever the hell they want. Women, we give up too easily, we are afraid of violence, we bury it, in and out of prison. Do you know how many women let a man beat her because she knows the cops won't help and she has nowhere to go? Same thing. We're trained to take what people dish out.

According to Alexandria, there were fewer options for women because they refused to use physical violence. Of course, men also explained that you must fight for everything you want in prison. In this sense, violence is described as a strategy for both men and women. The difference is that, for men, it is a more acceptable strategy. In fact, public displays of violence are expected because men are supposed to "fight" for their race. Women, however, denounce violent acts and must find other ways to resolve conflict.

In addition, women often stated that they did not have gang leaders in prison. Caroline explained why there were few gangs in women's prisons.

> CAROLINE: Women don't form gangs. Some women, the Mexican women, do some gangbanging. There are some Southerners and Northerners in women's prisons, but women in gangs is different. Women, you know, young girls do get involved in gangs in L.A. and Compton, but they do it to get with a guy. We all get involved with the bad boy, the guy that's going to get us into trouble. The thing is, in prison, there are no men to impress. There's just us and we don't get impressed with gang bangers. Now, we run drugs and stuff; I ran my fair share of drugs and I dated skinheads my whole life, but am I a skinhead? Not exactly, I just fuck them.

TRAMMELL: You don't see a lot of gang banging in prison?

CAROLINE: Some of the Mexican stuff, but it's not like the guys. We don't let it get out of hand. The men, they are all about gang banging. We're not into it.

Men often claimed that they joined gangs in prison because of racial segregation or for protection. Women, however, stated that some female inmates belong to gangs outside prison, but that did not necessarily affect their prison identity. The women in my study did not link race directly to gang membership. Also, they had no desire to force segregation like their male counterparts. Lupe discussed race relations and how she shared her cell with a variety of people:

I celled with whoever. They assigned me a black woman at first; okay, I can deal. I leave you alone, and you leave me alone. They gave me a white girl but she had some, you know, tattoos, the PENI shit, it pissed me off, so I tell her right off the bat that I don't roll that way, she wants the white power shit, fine, but keep it to yourself sister. She was fine, didn't say much. I prefer to be with another Chicana to be honest with you, but whatever; it's fine as long as they leave me be.

Several women made similar claims. They may have preferred segregation, but they followed the rules. Like the men, they noticed that women had gang tattoos (such as the PENI skinhead tattoos on Lupe's cellmate), and they identified many of the women by these tattoos, but, as Hayley stated, they didn't make much of them: "You know, a lot of women were in gangs but it wasn't a big deal. I knew women who ran with the Crips and stuff; they didn't get tats or anything. Some of the women got the NLR stuff or the Irish Pride crap; that's the skinheads. I didn't care and they didn't really act like anyone else." Karla told me how she learned not to judge people by their tattoos:

I knew this girl once, she had the Nazi stuff, the swastikas and she shaved her head and she was a tough-looking chick, let me tell you. She honestly scared me and I didn't want to be in the same room with her. One day, she sits by me in the yard and complains that we can't smoke any more. We talked about it for a while, and she told me about her kids and her girlfriend back home. She was real sweet and she had no problem talking to this black gal. You know, you can't judge a book by its cover. It made me want to talk to all kinds of women; they're okay in the long run, right?

Like other women I interviewed, Marilyn stated that she got her tattoos for her boyfriend's sake:

I got the PENI thing on my knuckles cuz I dated a guy that was into it. I don't really want to hang out with black chicks and stuff; I guess Mexicans are okay, some of them. My sister married a Mexican, he's nice. Some women commented on my tattoo; I got some looks and stuff. I kind of felt bad about it. I'm not ashamed or anything, but I didn't want to start anything, I just got it for Jimmy, you know?

Both Karla and Marilyn discussed how tattoos affect your public image in prison. In both of their stories, displays of skinhead ideology initially created problems. In Karla's story, the fact that a woman with Nazi tattoos reached out to her changed her perception about some of the women in prison. Although racist displays will offend some people and cause problems, it seems that these public displays do not necessarily cement your public image.

On the one hand, the men explained that gang affiliation was rather rigid as far as sharing a cell goes but, if gang leaders approve, flexible for playing cards or hanging around the yard. Women, on the other hand, seemed to be more interested in the character of the individual. If fellow inmates showed respect to one another, some of them can overlook these racist displays. In fact, Marilyn discussed the fact that she does not necessarily subscribe to a racist ideology. Instead, she aligned her actions with her skinhead boyfriend and hoped that she did not offend anyone.

Women also stated that they did not follow gang leaders like their male counterparts. At the same time, they often chose friends from their own cities. Tina explained how that usually happened.

TRAMMELL: Is race a problem for the women?

TINA: No it's not; it's more a problem of counties. Orange County people stick together and stuff.

TRAMMELL: Oh, it's by region?

TINA: Yeah, more so than anything. If anything happens, if there's any conflict, then you get with your homegirls from your area.

TRAMMELL: That's pretty standard to all the prisons you've seen?

TINA: Yeah, well, except Live Oak; it's a lot of white-collar crime so it's not the same, they just do their time and stuff.

TRAMMELL: Why do you think that women don't use the shot-caller system?

TINA: Women are too, um, striving for power; they are too catty. Everyone would want to be that star, so to speak. There's more of a formal system with the men; they assume their roles and they know their positions. With women, it's not like that.

TRAMMELL: There's no leadership position for the women?

TINA: No, there might be someone that stands out more than someone else, so they may defer to that person if there's some decisionmaking or whatever. You might ask that person what they think. There's not one person, no.

Hunt and his colleagues (1993:404) detailed how men in prison used to split up by region or area, but as the population grew, so did the number of gangs:

Previously, there were four or five major gangs; today there are nine or ten new groupings, each with its own networks and loyalties. These crosscutting and often conflicting allegiances have a significant impact on prison life. They produce a confusing, disruptive situation for many prisoners and can even produce problems for existing friendships.

As the number of men in prison increased, social networks were severed. Some men chose race as a dividing line. In other words, homeboys were originally from your hometown, but now members of your gang are homeboys. One key difference between men and women is the power given to prison gangs. Men come to identify with gangs in a way that divides them. There are gang members in women's prisons, but that does not necessarily affect their status there. Instead, as Mia explained, women relied on finding friends from their neighborhoods: "You're from L.A. or Riverside and stuff. Wherever you're from you usually end up hanging with those people. I'm from Anaheim, and so I hung out with other Orange County people and stuff. The men do it differently, but for me, I was fine if I was with my own girls." She did not use race as a factor in choosing friends. However, some women discussed class along with regional differences. For example, Marilyn made this comment about poor women living in Bakersfield:

I kid you not, if you'd hear about someone who never wore shoes as a kid or who was sleeping with their cousin and shit, they were always, I mean, always, from Bakersfield. I'm not sure what goes on up there, but shit, those girls are fucked up. We were from L.A., and we could always spot some poor, farm girl from Bakersfield. They were usually Mexican and dumb as dirt. I still laugh when I think of it.

Ella also describes hanging out with other women from her neighborhood.

ELLA: Race is interesting, we don't cell up like the guys; it's all about race for them. I'm from Compton, so yeah, I stuck with my girls from Compton, and there were plenty of them there. I actually knew a couple of girls from school. We mostly hang with ourselves. The Southerners and stuff, you know the Mexican girls from L.A., they hung out together. They were okay, I guess. We didn't mess with them, and they didn't mess with us.

TRAMMELL: What was their race?

ELLA: Black mostly, my neighborhood had mostly black families. Some Koreans but I never saw any Koreans in prison.

Of course, racial segregation is still quite common in US neighborhoods (Bobo and Zubrinsky 1996; Charles 2000; Krivo, Peterson, and Kuhl 2009; Massey and Denton 1993). If female inmates chose friends because of their zip code, they were likely to have friends of the same race.

One reason for the differences between male and female inmates' approach to race centers on the fact that their priorities are different. Men link segregation to control. They describe a battle with correctional officers about their ability to control their living arrangements. Women also want some control over their lives, but they are more concerned about the comfort and stability of their surroundings. Hayley summed up the differences between men and women:

It's very simple. Men want to hang with their own and sell their stuff. For men, it's all about who can make money. For women, it's different. We are mothers; we are wives. We go into prison and worry about our kids. Ask the men how often they worry about their children. They don't. We worry about the serious stuff, and they want to make money. They form their gangs to make money; it's that simple. For women, we just want someone to talk to and to help us get through the program.

Men certainly do want to make money in prison. Gangs become linked to these businesses when they divide up territory in the prison yard. Gangs are also racially identified, which helps facilitate the norms of segregation. For women, gangs represent a connection to people back home. In women's prisons, gang members probably do hang out together. For example, Ella stated that some of the Southerners were friends. However, the men and women I interviewed for this book differ with regard to the importance of gangs. Women care deeply about overcoming the indignities of prison. They try to find people who will help them through this process. That does not mean that race is never a problem for them.

Race and Violence

In men's prison, correctional officers are supposed to integrate the cells, but the men in my study explained that they resisted this process. The women told me they were more likely to follow directions, however. All the African American women in my study described racial integration as a good thing. However, 36 percent of women in my study (who were all white or Hispanic) explain that race was a serious problem in prison. Lupe had a fight with a woman who made advances on her prison girlfriend.

> LUPE: I got into a fight; we punched each other out over my girl. This new woman—it was a black woman, which pissed me off even more—she moves in on my girl. Well, first of all, my girl doesn't want any part of that. So I tell this chick to step off. She needs to bring it down a notch or two. She tells me that I can fuck off, I'm not telling her what to do. So we go at it.
>
> TRAMMELL: Where?
>
> LUPE: We were in a blind spot in the hallway; no one saw us, and I kicked her ass. She needed some dental work when I was done. I've been fighting since I was eleven years old; I know what I'm doing. The blacks think they're tough cuz they outnumber us, but they're all talk. When you get down to real business, they can't ever hold their own. Well, I held her own, let me tell you.

Olivia resented some of the African American women in prison:

> They [blacks] get very little in prison and think they are really rich since they have nothing on the outside. They tend to use their, well, they bully a lot of people. I was not one of them; I fought all the time. I was always fighting the black women because I'm not letting them get to me. They can't push me around. I was always a fighter; I'm a serious scrapper.

Emily had a similar story.

> EMILY: I had some black chicks that punched out one of my girls. Nothing sexual or anything, but we took it to the cell and took her down. She's not doing that with my girls.
>
> TRAMMELL: Did it make a difference that she was black?
>
> EMILY: Yes. They run the prisons; they think they're in charge. I don't like to be told who to run with. Like I said, I'm in charge. I'm not kissing ass or playing nice because the black bitches said so.

On average, 39 percent of women in California prisons are white, 29 percent are African American, and 28 percent are Hispanic (California Department of Corrections and Rehabilitation 2010). However, African Americans make up approximately 13 percent of the nonprison population (Humes, Jones, and Ramirez 2011). It is possible that white women believed African Americans outnumbered them in prison because there are a disproportionate number of African Americans in prison. Emily and Olivia blamed their problems on African Americans. More interesting, they stated that race affected prison culture when members of some races attempted to dominate others. Both women explained that African Americans' supposed domination inspired them to fight even harder. Unlike the men in this study, they do not claim to "fight for their race." Instead, race is a contributing factor because they blame women of another race for their own lack of power.

In recent years, scholars have shown that incarcerated women can, and do, commit acts of violence (Alarid 2000; Greer 2000; Trammell 2009a). For example, according to Kimberly R. Greer (2000:464), "the social environment described by the women in this prison is similar in nature to that portrayed in literature pertaining to male correctional institutions." In my interviews, I learned that race matters for both men and women. However, the women were not fighting for segregation. Also, they were somewhat divided on this issue: the majority of the women I interviewed enjoyed their relationships with women of all races.

Others, like Hannah, described racial segregation as the ideal type of social organization because it is what men do.

> The guys said we would go in and separate by race. I'd roll with my own cars, but that's not what happened. Instead I was told that we don't play that race card in prison and that we all had to get along. Women are supposed to be different or something; we can't act like men. Well, I do think that women are better than men, but I should be able to hang with my own. I don't equate better than men with hanging with the blacks. I punched a black woman once, and you'd have thought I punched out the pope. It's like they're off limits. This is what happens when they force us to cell up with them.

Rosa's husband also went to prison, and he told her that segregation was the norm:

> ROSA: Women like to cell up with their own. Most women will complain that guards cell us with someone we don't like.
>
> TRAMMELL: Based on race?

ROSA: Yeah, sometimes. My husband said he celled up with Mexicans in prison, and that's what I thought we'd do. I've never lived with white or black women, you know? I was real surprised about it. No one says anything, but women bitch about it all the time. I think they'd prefer doing it like the guys do.

It seems logical that women would talk to others who served time in prison about what to expect. Lucy, like Rosa, was surprised that the norms differed so much between men and women.

My cousin went to prison. He would sit around for hours telling us about that stuff. Mostly funny stuff, and he'd get pissed if we asked him if he ever got raped. The first time I went in, I'm like, this isn't what I thought would happen. We all celled up with all kinds of women, and women aren't that funny. I was ready to fight, but there wasn't a lot to fight about. I never knew a lot of black women, you know? I really didn't know any before I went to prison. My mom used to tell us that blacks were crazy; well, there were plenty of crazy black women in prison, that's for sure. When I got out, I told my cousin that women do it different. The second time I went in, I was fine. I was all ready for it because I went through it before and that prepared me for the second and third time I went in.

Although race is a defining characteristic, it is not as problematic for women due to the norms of civility. When faced with conflict, inmates understand their choices of action. Although Hannah, Rosa, and Lucy believed that segregation was the norm, they did not fight with correctional officers, and they did not try to force women to segregate. Instead, they resented African American women.

If you remember, 75 percent of the men in my study had friends of different races. At the same time, 64 percent of the women in my study described integration as a good thing. The others explained that they simply did not want friends and cellies of different races but were forced to do so because of official rules and informal norms. They might fight with other inmates and blame race as a contributing factor. However, they were not willing to go to extreme measures to segregate their cells. They might blame and resent African American women for "bossing them around," but they would not start a race riot.

Female inmates explained that women were limited in their strategies because they would not use violence. As Swidler (1986) pointed out, our actions are tied to our cultural norms. There is no doubt that men commit more violence than women in prison (California Department of Corrections and Rehabilitation 2007). What is interesting is that male inmates explained that violence was often used instrumentally to get something they want, such as segregation. In this sense, violence was a more acceptable "strategy of action" for men than women. Women who used violence as a strategy often stated that they did so despite the norm of racial harmony.

Conclusion

On the surface, it appears that men do not (racially) mix while women do. However, on closer inspection, we see that men sometimes have friends of different races and will sell their illegal products to anyone. Many women denounce segregation and describe the virtues of a civilized culture of racial integration. However, 36 percent of the women I interviewed claimed to have fought about race while incarcerated. Violence, as a strategy, appears to be more acceptable for men. Also, men obey the norm of segregation in a way that actually unites them against the prison staff. Women, however, appear to be less united about this issue.

It seems that racism was not the sole reason why men, and some women, desired racial segregation. There were racist overtones in their stories, and some people were not embarrassed about their racist language or attitudes. At the same time, both men and women were quite angry about living in prison. Race served as an acceptable way to create alliances as men and women learned the rules of their environment and tried to fit in. They could not control the fact that the state was telling them where to sleep, what to eat, when to work, and so forth. Controlling race relations gave them some say over their lives. For men, this was especially easy when the California Department of Corrections and Rehabilitation segregated the inmates by race. Now that official rules have changed, the men were upset about the possible changes in their daily routines.

To change this rule violates an informal agreement among inmates and may cause anger and violence to be aimed at prison staff. Male inmates interpreted efforts to desegregate as a loss of power and a disruption of their informal norms. Unfortunately for correctional officers and other prison staff, violence is one strategy of action for incarcerated men. I do not mean to say that inmates will take over these prisons and gain back their right to segregate. There is a good chance that the inmates will be the ones to suffer for rebelling against desegregation.

From a cultural perspective, some interesting themes about race and violence have emerged from these interviews. Cultural norms about race and interpersonal relationship influence how people act despite their own personal values. Furthermore, comparisons of the stories told by men and women show some similarities. One is that white men and women complained about losing their majority status in prison, which led them to blame the out-groups (Hispanics and African Americans) for their troubles. Sometimes the blaming escalated to violence for both men and women.

The majority of people I interviewed stated that they had no problem with people of other races. Yet, the men adhered to the norms of segregation in prison despite their beliefs. In what seems like a contradiction, they stated that the fluid nature of these rules allowed them to deal drugs to anyone and have some friends of other races. For women, cultural norms promoted racial integration, but some women fought about race. Cultural norms did not necessarily constrain their behavior entirely. Instead, inmates worked to create what Stowell and Byrne (2008) called a "worthy identity" because their performance must be acceptable to other inmates.

Publicly, both men and women followed the prescribed norms about residential segregation in prison. Despite cultural breaches where their own values influenced their behavior despite cultural norms, they maintained a positive public identity. These were not intentional breaches per se. Interviewees were not trying to change prison culture or start social movements in prison. They described culture as solid but worked to sidestep some of the norms. For example, if white men wanted to play cards with African Americans, they could explain that they did so to take their money, which made it acceptable to fellow gang members and shot-callers.

The fact that rival skinhead gangs created alliances with Hispanic or African American gangs indicates that the racial divide is not that clear-cut. Also, it indicates that culture is an ongoing process that is influenced by many factors. Things such as underground businesses, new prison gangs, and other factors will affect how inmates interact with each other. These cultural breaches will also shape prison culture as informal rules change, or relax, in response to the behavior of incoming inmates.

The key is to maintain a valid performance. Male and female inmates can step around the informal norms to some degree, but they risk retaliation, including violence, if they oppose them outright. If men decide to fight against men of their own race during a race riot, they are marked. Their public displays must show that they are committed to informal rules. Public actions are especially important for the men for two reasons. First, to outwardly oppose segregation aligns their actions with the goals of the prison administration. Obviously, that is not an option. Second, violence is an acceptable response for these men. For women, violence is less acceptable. This does not mean that they never fight. In fact, several women in my study fought others in prison. Some of these women stated that they would have preferred segregation. However, the norms surrounding acceptable behavior for incarcerated women tied their hands.

4

Gender, Sex, and Rape

A lot of the research on prison rape and gender focuses on men, masculinity, and sexual abuse (Donaldson 2001, 2003; Kupers 2001; Parenti 1999; Pinar 2001). For example, Stephen Donaldson (2003) outlines how heterosexual men cope with being raped in prison. Some men choose a decent person to hook up with, which Donaldson calls "protective pairing." In these relationships, the dominant male protects the weaker, feminized male and demands oral and/or anal sex in return. The dominant man retains his manhood, whereas the prison "punk" is demoted to female and used for sexual gratification (Donaldson 2003:348); however, being "punked out" is preferable to other options:

> One reason why this custom has survived for so long is that the alternatives for the known rape victim are usually even more unacceptable. These are a series of very serious and bloody fights, and maybe a lot more time; suicide (a permanent "solution" to a temporary problem); repeated exposure to gang-rapes; paying someone for protection; and permanent consignment to "protective custody" in Seg. This last option, p.c., may not even be safe, staff may not allow you to stay there indefinitely, and solitary can drive you crazy if endured for too long.

Studies on women focus on the fact that many women have lesbian relationships in prison (Bowker 1977; Clark 1995; Forsyth, Evans, and Foster 2002; Hampton 1993; Leger 1987; Propper 1982). Researchers have found that women need a strong social support system while incarcerated (Toch 2002; Toch and Adams 1989), so they make friends

65

and create families (Chesney-Lind 2002; MacKenzie, Robinson, and Campbell 1989; Pollock 1998). Female inmates typically have children, are unmarried, have a long history of victimization, and are more likely to be incarcerated for nonviolent offenses (Chesney-Lind 2002; Child Welfare League of America 2003; Owen 1998; Pollock and Davis 2005). Finding friends, girlfriends, or a family in prison is a way to cope with the pain of incarceration and the separation from their families. Owen (1998) found that fights between girlfriends are more common than fights between strangers in women's prisons. Women sometimes fight because of sexual jealousy.

Unfortunately, abusive relationships between female inmates and correctional officers have been documented (Burton-Rose 2003; Human Rights Watch 2001; Human Rights Watch Women's Rights Project 1996; Smith 1998; Talvi 2003). Lawsuits filed on behalf of sexually abused women have resulted in millions of dollars paid to victims in these cases (Burton-Rose 2003). Also, there is some evidence of sexual abuse between female inmates. Leanne Fiftal Alarid (2000) studied letters from a female inmate and found sexual abuse between inmates may appear consensual, depending on how questions are asked or whether or not inmates labeled specific acts as abuse. She also found that sexual coercion, when ignored by prison staff, is likely to escalate into more serious acts of violence.

In addition, she developed a classification system of female aggressors in which the "Stud" role is played by African American and lesbian women and the "Jailhouse Femme" role is taken by women of all races who engage in sexual relationships. Her findings were limited in that she relied on letters from one inmate. However, her research provided new insight into female aggression and came out at the same time as Greer's (2000:452) study of sexual relationships in women's prisons. According to Greer, "Involvement in these relationships may not be as pervasive as previously discovered and when formed, may be initiated for different reasons. Findings from this study also suggest that these respondents believe sexual relationships are based primarily on manipulation rather than on any perception of compatibility or genuine attraction between partners." The women in her study did not believe most sexual relationships develop because women wanted to comfort each other. Instead, many relationships formed for economic reasons. Some women had money or other material goods, and her respondents discussed how "canteen whores" had sex with women to gain access to these things. Greer's interviewees detailed how sexual relationships had little to do with romantic attachment, which contradicts many studies on incarcerated women, but they did not mention a classification system like Alarid's (Stud, Jailhouse Femme).

Prison Culture and Rape

Fleisher and Kreinert (2009) disputed the idea that prison rape is an epidemic. Their study explored the nuances of prison culture from the perspective of the inmates. They found that there are many "myths" surrounding prison rape and inmate sexuality: "There are no studies in the vast literature on prison culture that acknowledge humans' sexual flexibility. In all-male and all-female prisons the absence of heterosexual partners may establish cultural conditions that allow the expression of homosexual sex, but the proximal causal factor is cultural sexual malleability (25–26)." Researchers sometimes misinterpret same-sex relations in prisons as sexual abuse (Fleisher and Kreinert 2009). Not only do researchers need to acknowledge the continuum of human sexuality, but also they need to better understand inmate culture in order to understand these relationships.

To be sure, people outside prison increasingly view prison rape as a problem. Lawmakers passed the Prison Rape Elimination Act in 2003 and the California Sexual Abuse in Detention Elimination Act, which stipulates zero tolerance for sexual abuse in prison, in 2005. Despite estimates from the Prison Rape Elimination Act, a few researchers find that rape is rare and consensual sex is quite common. According to Fleisher and Kreinhert (2009), some men find their "inner homosexual" (74) in prison. In addition, they stated, "Acts of sexual violence are not rape unless those acts meet particular conditions set by inmate culture's construction of rape" (85). In other words, inmate culture dictates whether inmates define specific acts as rape. Once inmates define what is, or is not, rape, men are less likely to call some acts "rape" or "sexual abuse" because they believe that these acts are consensual.

For example, let's say that a male prisoner approaches a victim of physical or sexual abuse and offers to protect him as long as they have sex. If the victim agrees because he does not want to be raped or beaten, prisoners would probably not label this behavior as sexual abuse. Others would call this protective pairing and describe it as a form of sexual violence (Donaldson 2003; Kupers 2001). To be sure, if a man approaches a rape victim outside prison and tells her that he will let men rape her again unless she has sex with him, that would be defined as sexual abuse. The norms surrounding prison rape and prison sex differ from sexual activity outside prison. The social construction of the convicted felon allows many people to believe that inmates deserve to be mistreated. More important to this argument is the fact that prisons have their own distinct cultures, which, at times, directly conflict with the norms of the nonprison world.

Some researchers claim that no one is raped in prison; others say that up to 40 percent of inmates are raped (Gaes and Goldberg 2004). In a study of sexual assault in both men's and women's prisons, Cindy Struckman-Johnson and her colleagues (1996) found that 22.0 percent of men and 7.7 percent of women reported being pressured and/or forced into sexual acts. This study documented one of the highest rates of sexual assault for female inmates. However, in conducting their study, the researchers mailed questionnaires to inmates, who mailed the survey back in a prepaid envelope. This method, although convenient, creates a problem with reliability (Gaes and Goldberg 2004). Furthermore, their low response rate of 28.7 percent ($N = 516$) indicates inmates may have been pressured not to respond. In sum, it is difficult to evaluate how many men and women are sexually assaulted in US prisons.

The Rules of Prison Sex

The men and women in my study described rape and sexual abuse as a thing of the past. Men explained that rape was a serious problem in the early years of mass incarceration but that in recent years, rape almost never happens. Women told me sexual abuse was not a problem in women's prisons. They also described prison culture as hypersexual, however, which coincides with Fleisher and Kreinert's (2009) research about prison culture. Interviewees stated that inmates talk about sex, masturbate, and have sex with each other quite often. Several men told me that sex is happening all around the prison, and women talked about how they went "gay for the stay" while incarcerated.

I first asked interviewees why prison rape was underreported. All but one told me that rape was not a problem in prison. They stated that inmates often have consensual sex; therefore, rape was not needed for sexual gratification. Ronald told me: "If men are fucking in prison, they're fucking by choice. No rape. You have no idea; men hook up all the time. I know that rape happens; I know of some men who got it in prison, but you have to understand, all men do in prison is talk about sex, jerk off, or do each other. I've seen guys giving head all over the place. Rape? No, it's not a problem."

Ethan told me this story:

> Yeah, I knew of guys who would come in all tough and macho and shit
> and in a year or so, they would get with the program. I knew a guy
> who had sex in prison and would tell me, "Hey, I'm here for ten years;
> you think I'm not getting head?" This was a black dude! It's not even
> like they are on the down-low; they just give up and say, "Fuck it, I'm
> having sex." It happens more than you think.

Of all of the men in my study, none of them claimed to have been
raped or to have had sex in prison. However, all the men claimed that
everyone else was having sex. They told me that it happens so often that
most men get caught by other inmates. They also said that prison was a
very sexual place to live. Men discussed sex more than anything else.
Evan had this to say:

> It's strange; men talk about sex all the time, right? If I'm hanging out
> with some friends, we'll start talking about getting some, right? In
> prison, it's a million times worse. I remember having this . . . four-
> hour conversation about . . . pussy and breasts and stuff. We talked
> about what we liked, how it tasted, and I was hard the whole time. I
> finally told the guy that we had to stop; it hurts, you know what I
> mean? Well, think about doing that all damn day, every day. It is like
> torture. They put us in a place where there are only men and expect us
> to what, knit? No, we drive each other crazy talking about how much
> our girls like to fuck.

According to Evan and Ethan, prison was a hypersexual environment. Fleisher and Kreinert put it this way (2009:66): "Prison sexuality
represents a complex socio-cultural network with increasingly fluid sexual roles." In other words, you can engage in homosexual acts and still
identify as straight. Sex was used for gratification, and same-sex relationships were common. However, Anthony told me that homosexual
acts could alter your public identity.

> A lot of guys do it in prison. They say that they have sex because they
> have to and they are straight when they get out. I think that's bullshit.
> Let me tell you, if you have sex with a guy, you are gay. It's plain and
> simple. Me and my boys, we knew they were full of shit and we'd laugh
> at them. I got nothing against gays; I have them in my family. This isn't
> about being a homophobe. This is about a basic, biological fact. If you
> have sex with a guy, you're gay. Just be gay and get over it.

Male inmates were not necessarily concerned about homosexuality
but about deception. Angelo had this to say: "There are a ton of fags in

prison. There are also guys who say they're not gay but suck dick. Look, there is a guy code; if you don't want to be gay, you don't suck dick. Going to prison doesn't change that." Angelo described the norms of masculinity and how men could not breach these norms without altering their image. Gil, in contrast, felt that homosexuality was wrong and should not be tolerated.

> GIL: I know of a lot of guys who hooked up in prison; not for me. You know, most of the guys do it after they've been there a while. I don't think that people do it right off the bat. They just, you know, get horny after a while, like six months or so, and they cave. Don't ask me to explain it; if my boys pulled that shit, we'd check them.
>
> TRAMMELL: So, no one in your gang had sex?
>
> GIL: We didn't have any fags, I mean gays, in my group. If you do that, you are gay. I did fifteen years and I never had sex once; it is not hard. No one dies because they don't have sex. If they are having sex, it's because they want to have sex with men.

Clearly, such statements are grounded in homophobia.

Despite the prison culture in which heterosexual men have sex with other men while "staying straight," these men argued that the act itself meant something. Of course, they told me this after they left prison. They may have been less shocked about these relationships in prison. Fleisher and Kreinert (2009:66) argued that that there are two "sexual tracks" in prison. One track includes homosexual men having sex in prison, and the "second track contains men who define themselves as straight, but may or may not participate in sexual acts with other men. Regardless of their behavior, they are seen as heterosexual by members of the prison culture."

It is entirely possible that sex is so common in prison that some men have sex and still maintain a heterosexual identity. It seems that prison, as a hypersexual environment, does not overtly discourage homosexual encounters. As others have shown, men adhere to their prescribed gender norms, especially about sex and sexuality (Bourdieu 2001; McGuffey and Rich 1999; Pollack 1999; Thorne 1993, 1998). To be sure, fraternity houses and high school locker rooms are also filled with young men obsessed with sex. However, the norm of heterosexuality is also strictly enforced in these environments. Not everyone believes that you can engage in same-sex relations and be straight at the same time.

Rape and Protective Pairing

Of course, there are subcultures in prison, including a homosexual sub-culture, which some men are forced into. Fleisher and Kreinert (2009) explained how men are violently turned out, which means that a man is physically forced to have sex. Once this happens, he is usually victim-ized again because he is targeted for being too weak to protect himself. After that, inmates will usually not call it rape. Fleisher and Kreinert in-terviewed one man who was attacked by a rapist who choked him, wres-tled with him, and refused to take no for an answer. He repeatedly told his victim that he was going to penetrate him and fought him until the victim was exhausted. The victim finally said, "Fuck, OK" and stopped fighting him off.

> After he got finished, he sat down and talked to me and stuff like that. I was so angry and couldn't do nothing about it; emotionally it really messed me up. It's still a rape; there's nothing I can do about it. When I got out in [the] general population, I was turned out. There wasn't no beating; he choked me at first to get me, but after I submitted the rape itself wasn't aggressive. He didn't continue to choke me while pene-trating or nothing like that, he made me feel comfortable. (Fleisher and Kreinert 2009:103)

The fact that the man stopped fighting off his aggressor and said that he was made to "feel comfortable" meant that what happened would not be interpreted as an aggressive act (Fleisher and Kreinert 2009:102). In other words, when he stopped fighting, he joined the homosexual sub-culture. Several of my interviewees described men who were forced to have sex with other men for protection. The victims were usually blamed for not being tough enough to fight off an attacker. Eduardo told me that real men are not raped. He believed that weaker men volunteer for sex in order to be protected:

> EDUARDO: I'm telling you, men don't want anyone to hold them in prison, right? I mean, I knew men that got raped in prison and I know of men that—what's a good word for it—volunteered, that's not the right word, but I guess they volunteered to fuck guys in prison because they thought they'd get taken care of. Does that make sense? I don't know if these guys were really homos or not. I just know that they didn't care about fucking these guys since they get something out of it. If I told you [speaking to me] that you had to fuck me or I'll let another guy stab you, you'd call it rape,

right? In prison, it's just business. These guys are so fucked up that they don't see it. Also, I'd hear guys say that men "don't get raped; bitches get raped but not us." What are they? Stupid? That really freaked me out.

TRAMMELL: You think people volunteer for this?

EDUARDO: More like accepting. Some men accept their place in prison, trust me, it's not a lot of guys; most get with the program, toughen up, take no shit, demand respect—all that stuff. But you come across some of these guys that put up with being someone's punk for protection.

Eduardo, along with many other men, explained that these relationships are akin to a business agreement. Men "accepted" their role as prison punks and gained protection for doing so. Of course, Eduardo also pointed out that, if these men had been tough enough to take care of themselves, they would not be coerced into sex. A common theme emerging in these interviews was that men were often blamed for not being tough enough or masculine enough to fight their own battles in prison. Men often blamed each other for not living up to the expected norms of masculinity. In doing so, they always pointed out that rape could never happen to them. Carlos told me that men can always fight off an attacker, "There are all kinds of guys in prison; there are the straight-out gay dudes who come in gay and hook up. Some guys, they turn in prison. I mean, they don't fight back, right? If some guy jumps me, do you think I'm giving it up? Look, toughen up or don't, but don't puss out and call it rape, cuz it isn't rape." Interviewees knew that inmates would wear someone out with physical challenges but did not call it rape. Instead, the victim was blamed for being ignorant of this trick. In fact, they seemed to be more willing to call sexual violence "rape" if they knew less about the incident. Several men admitted they knew of some rape victims in prison. Austin told me this story:

AUSTIN: You know, I heard a guy screaming once, either he was being raped or tortured or something. He was yelling for help and stuff. I don't know what happened to him. Hell, I don't even know who it was. We were in our cells, so I just heard a voice.

TRAMMELL: He was just yelling for help?

AUSTIN: Yeah, it shook me up. I assumed he was being raped. Nothing ever came out of it; no one responded. The thing is, once you are marked, that's it; there's no going back. You get hit once and the same guy is going to do you over and over; other guys too. The first time is real violent, but the violence stops after that and the guy just gets passed around.

Kory explained how to distinguish rape from other attacks overheard in prison:

> You hear men scream or something. You can tell that it's not just some guy screwing around. You know the difference. If no one is being stabbed, then it might be rape. If someone is jumped and stabbed or killed, they'll lock down the prison, and everyone knows who got hit. If nothing happens, then it's probably rape. If guys get with someone, that's different; everyone knows who's doing that. If you hear a guy scream and you don't ever hear anything else, it's probably rape.

Austin and Kory made several interesting points. First, they implied that there were no secrets in prison. Information traveled fast. Second, they assumed that men were being raped when they screamed for help. Finally, what happens after the initial sexual contact mattered. If men were attacked and then continued a relationship with their attacker (protective pairing), then it became a legitimate agreement.

Several interviewees explained that if you were raped in prison, it was best to stay quiet about it. Eduardo gave this example: "Yeah, this guy on my block was raped; some guy took him on in his cell. I wasn't there when it happened. Everyone was talking about it, though; he was jumped pretty hard. This guy had no friends before or after it happened. It's like, you're done if that happens to you. It's better if no one ever finds out about it." If you recall, the men in my study claimed that rape was not a problem. At the same time, they told stories about anonymous men who were raped in prison. They told me that men screamed out for help, and they called that rape. Nevertheless, they maintained that rape was not a problem.

When I asked them to clarify this issue, they stated that they themselves could not be raped. In other words, rape was not a problem in prison because men "gave up" and stopped fighting; that meant they were not raped. Rape was only a problem for those who were not tough enough to avoid being assaulted, as Miguel indicated: "Rape is not a problem. Do you think that someone could rape me? I would take a bullet first. There are guys having sex; that's a fact. This is not rape. It is like a marriage; everyone is happy about it. If they're being raped, why aren't they fighting back?" Male inmates often blame the victim for refusing to live up to a masculine ideal. Ian explained why it is important to "toughen up" in prison: "The trick is to toughen up. You have to maintain while in prison. Lift weights, get in a few fights, maybe beat some guys down. Take no shit from anyone. That's what I did; no one fucked with me cuz they knew I wasn't going to take it." Eduard, Miguel, and

Ian were enunciating the informal rules of prison, which they understood as being protective. Those who do not accept these rules immediately might fall into traps set by fellow inmates.

Oscar described one of the ways that men are punked out: "I knew some people, some white guys, they talked about how you can get a guy to wear down, tire him out and shit. You know, like make him do thirty push-ups, dare him to a push-up contest, and let him go first. Then he gets tired, and he's easy to take on. Tired or not, no guy is sticking it to me. Maybe they want it all along, but it's less gay or something this way." James explained how roughhousing might be used to wear out the men:

> A lot of the guys in prison will hump you in the yard, you know, run up and pretend to hump you. Everyone laughs; they grab your junk and shit; it's just screwing around. I had a guy take it too far once, tried to wrestle me; I think he was seeing if I was into it. I had to beat him down and show him who's boss. You have to know how these guys manipulate the situation and shit. The cons are good at pretending to be your friend cuz they want something.

Some men stated that this horseplay was innocent, whereas some said that it was used to tire someone out or test them to see if they were serious about having sex.

One point that interested me was that these men believed that rape could be prevented. The real problem was not rape but weakness. Even the men who described real victims of rape called these victims weak. At the same time, male inmates despised all sex offenders, including men who attacked others in prison. For example, Jose stated: "If you are raping another guy in prison, you are sick. There's plenty of head in prison; there is no need to take someone by force. We hated those guys too; they are not in the same camp as the guys who rape kids, but they deserve everything they get."

Sex offenders were often despised by inmates and were relegated to the bottom of the prison hierarchy (Fleisher and Krienert 2009; Trammell and Chenault 2009). However, the victim was often described in negative terms as well. Obviously, prison culture is greatly influenced by the norms of masculinity: If you are tough, you are respected. If you show any weakness, you drop within the social hierarchy. Many described sexual relationships in prison as starting with violence but ending with sex. Only 18 percent of the men in my study claimed that same-sex relationships were wrong because they do not like homosexuals. This type of relationship was not described as violent or coercive;

it was simply a sexual relationship. However, no one described it as a loving or caring relationship. It was about sex, plain and simple.

These findings coincide with Fleisher and Krienert's (2009) study on prison culture, with one exception: the men in my study said that these sexual behaviors did imply that the participants are gay. Of course, I interviewed men who were out of prison, where the norms surrounding sex differed from those of the prison environment. That could have affected how they responded to my interview questions. These men described norms in a way that painted them in the best light: that is why they described everyone having sex in prison but them.

There is no doubt that inmates participated in this culture and used these stories to describe the norms of prison and prison sex. Fleisher and Kreinert (2009) are correct when they say that the stories or myths of prison rape teach inmates about prison culture (i.e., do not accept gifts from strangers). They serve as a warning about how to survive in prison. In addition, these stories describe norms about gender and power. To be sure, inmates entering prison understand the norms surrounding gender roles. In the subculture of prison, however, norms are greatly influenced by the same-sex environment and the confines of the total institution. Same-sex relationships were mostly tolerated and, according to these men, quite common in prison, unlike in the nonprison world, which is still influenced by homophobic norms. It seems, on the surface, that prison culture is more tolerant of these relationships than nonprison culture.

However, the fact that inmates refused to acknowledge that some of these acts are abusive tells us something else. During research for the Prison Rape Elimination Act, California inmates who admitted to being sexually abused or assaulted were asked about the reason for the attack. The modal response was that the attack was about sex. In their sample, 63.3 percent of sexually assaulted men in the non-transgender sample said that the incident was sex-related, and 10 percent said it was about power and control. In the transgender population, 37 percent of those who were sexually abused or assaulted stated it was sex-related, and 12.3 percent said it was about power and control (Jenness et al. 2007).

The men in my study also said that rape was simply about sex. Therefore, the argument that no one is raped in prison because sex is so common makes perfect sense. If rape is about sex and sex is readily available, men are probably less likely to report rape. Also, men stated that rape victims were better off not reporting the rape. Those who did were "marked" as victims and lost friends, putting them at risk of further abuse. They can let others take care of them and exchange sex for this protection. In any event, rape was likely to be underreported because of these informal norms.

If sexual abuse happened, inmates labeled these men in accordance with established prison norms. They constructed a narrative that focused on sexual gratification and strength. Fleisher and Kreinert (2009:5) described rape myths as "a collection of culturally rational narratives that have knowledge fundamental to the culture itself." These myths function to disseminate information about prison norms. These stories warned others about the importance of staying strong and maintaining the peace.

I agree with Fleisher and Kreinert (2009) when they point out that a lot of research on prison rape is tainted by the fact that many people, including researchers, are so shocked by same-sex relationships that they describe an "epidemic" of prison rape. However, I also contend that it is equally shocking that we have come so far in our efforts to prevent the rape of women, yet rape myths are so common in prison. If we substituted "women" for "inmates" in any of these stories, we would probably not excuse these acts in the name of cultural relevance. However, there were no antirape or feminist movements in prison. Instead, we have overcrowded prisons and fewer rehabilitative programs.

It is highly likely that these men, along with other inmates, never even thought about being a victim of sexual assault. That simply was not their lived reality. Once incarcerated, they had to face the fact that they could be sexually assaulted, which probably accounted for their too-quick explanations that rape was not a problem in prison. They felt compelled to convince me, and anyone who would listen, that they were never in danger in prison. And to buttress their argument, they redefined acts of sexual assault as something else. In order to do that, they focused particularly on the victim: he did not fight back, or he was overpowered. That is not the behavior of a real man. That is the behavior of a victim.

This is not to say that they blamed all victims of rape. They clearly despised rapists and child molesters (Trammell and Chenault 2009). However, they could not or would not identify with men who were sexually abused. If they labeled most cases of rape as sex, it completely redefined the relationship between attacker and victim. It was especially interesting to me that these men used the norms of masculinity to define these behaviors. By doing so, they attempted to show how men control their environment in prison. They minimized the effects of abuse by blaming the victim.

Going "Gay for the Stay" in Women's Prison

As previous studies indicate, women engage in transitional lesbianism in prison (Bowker 1977; Clark 1995; Forsyth, Evans, and Foster 2002; Hampton 1993; Leger 1987; Propper 1982). The women in my study called this going "gay for the stay." I asked about these relationships, and women often told me that homosexual relationships take the place of heterosexual ones. Relationships were very important to these women, and they described the benefits of having friends in prison. Also, women were very forthcoming about these relationships: there is no shame associated with having a prison girlfriend, as Molly stated: "Well, women get with each other in prison [laughs]; they end up getting girlfriends. It's called 'gay for the stay.' You can only date and have sex with men until you get to prison and then all of a sudden, you're a lesbian." The term "gay for the stay" implies the relationship is temporary. Women resumed heterosexual relationships once they left prison. Sofia explained that these relationships are grounded in friendship:

> TRAMMELL: What's it mean to be gay for the stay?
>
> SOFIA: It means that you go into prison or jail and you hook up with some woman. You and her become girlfriends.
>
> TRAMMELL: And sex is a part of this?
>
> SOFIA: Yes, but it's also about having a best friend and such.

These relationships helped women cope with incarceration. Rosa described her girlfriend as her best friend: "Women get with each other because they are lonely. They get to talk with someone, have someone to complain to. They get to have a new best friend. Prison is a lonely place; if you don't have friends, you will die inside. A girlfriend helps fill you up; she gives you a reason to live. I still talk to my girl from prison. She and I are still good friends."

In fact, as Olivia explained, not having a girlfriend meant that no one wanted you.

> When women come into prison they say, "Oh, my God, how could you do that? Why would you get with a woman?" But the curiosity is there; it's always there. Even the women that are freaked about it at first end up with someone. It could be needing somebody; it could be the sexual part of it all or just the curiosity. It's very uncommon to find a woman that's not with someone. If they are, it's because no one wants to be with them.

Edith agreed that some women in prison were unpopular and lonely "I knew women in prison, they had no friends, I mean no friends. These women didn't want friends, and no one wanted to be with them. They had no girlfriends, that's for sure. We used to laugh about this one girl and dare each other to get close with her. It's like, 'hey, you should get her as your girlfriend.' It became the big joke."

Although none of my male interviewees admitted to having had sex in prison, 27 percent of the women I interviewed were open about it. Unlike men, who categorized these relationships as outlets for sexual gratification only, women described these relationships in positive terms. They told me that these women were their best friends and lovers.

Previous research has found that men and women adhered to their prescribed gender norms, especially about sex and sexuality (Bourdieu 2001; McGuffey and Rich 1999; Pollack 1999; Thorne 1993, 1998). Men blamed weak men for failing to be tough in prison and not avoiding rape, and women made fun of inmates who could not get girlfriends. For women, the relationship itself mattered. Aura told me that she loved her girlfriend.

> TRAMMELL: Describe the types of sexual relationships in prison. Did you have a girlfriend?
>
> AURA: Sure, we all did. My girlfriend was my best friend. I was closer to her than anyone else. It wasn't like my boyfriends, we were like sisters. I love her.

Prudence described how much she needed to be with someone while she was in prison:

> TRAMMELL: Did you have a girlfriend in prison?
>
> PRUDENCE: Oh, yeah, I think everyone does. I lost my kids, my boyfriend; my folks will never talk with me again. I knew that going in. My girlfriend, she stood by me. I got to be with the best person on earth. I really needed her, and we stuck to each other. It was for comfort; I really needed to be with someone, I still love her.

Going to prison is an emotional, terrifying experience, and not just for women. Men are terrified as well; they describe men who scream for help during an attack. Yet of all the men I interviewed, not one used the term "love" to describe these relationships. Gender norms make it acceptable for women to feel weak and vulnerable, which allows them to reach out to others in a more functional manner and to make connections with one another.

Sexual Violence in Women's Prisons

Although most women described the positive side of these relationships, others spoke of how some women dominated their girlfriends. Women categorized these relationships as a type of protective pairing (Donaldson 2001, 2003; Kupers 2001) in which a smaller (or younger) woman found a dominating woman to hook up with. These women are terrified about the prison experience and end up being taken care of but must concede power to the dominant partner. In these relationships, the dominant woman usually controls the weaker one sexually. Within my study, 30 percent of the women I interviewed knew of someone in a violent prison relationship. Emily explained how some women were punished if they refused to have sex with their girlfriends.

> EMILY: Look, if you say you're going to do me or someone else, then you better get with the program. Don't put yourself out there if you're not going through with it.
>
> TRAMMELL: Put yourself out there, what do you mean?
>
> EMILY: I'm just saying that you get what you get if you put yourself out there.
>
> TRAMMELL: Give me an example of what you mean, something you saw in prison.
>
> EMILY: Okay, I knew this woman, and she said she was a dyke. She got a girlfriend, a pretty tough chick, and this woman took care of her, right? Okay, push comes to shove and the little gal, she backs out. Says she really likes guys and can't go through with going down on a woman. Not cool. You got to get with the program or shut up. You got the benefits, right? You got a girlfriend, you're safe with her, she's taking care of you, and now you don't want to get down. Wrong move, bitch. This woman who said she was a dyke really wasn't one. Her then ex-girlfriend got her girls to hold her down and fuck her with a hot curling iron. That's what happens if you put yourself out there. Just be honest; it's the lying that pisses us off.
>
> TRAMMELL: So they raped her?
>
> EMILY: I would not call that rape. Rape is something else. You can't get someone pumped up, you know, get someone ready for action, and then back out. There's a way to do things, and the right way is to

go with the program. If you're getting the benefits, you gotta put out. It's not rape under any circumstance.

She told me that women volunteered for these relationships in order to find protection. If those women refused to have sex, then violence ensued. That is very similar to the stories told by men. In both cases, the underlying problem was the fact that an inmate was getting a service and not holding up his or her end of the bargain. Both men and women explained that rape was wrong but prison sex was rarely rape. In other words, inmates gave up their right to consent if they entered into a deal with other inmates. Prison culture demands that inmates keep their word to one another. Those who backed out of agreements were at risk for retaliation.

Much like their male counterparts, women explained that the dominant woman had the power in those relationships. Hayley told me some of the details:

Well, some of the women are a little weaker than the others, the weak ones . . . you know, the ones that are smaller or young and stuff, they usually try to hook up with a bigger woman or a woman that's been in prison for a while, and then the bigger woman takes care of the little woman and she's her girlfriend. Sometimes the older woman just tries to take care of the younger woman because some of the women prey on some of the younger women. It's kind of a zoo in there. Sometimes little women get ganged up on, and so they will look for someone to protect them. There's no men in there, so they have to take care of each other.

As pointed out in Chapter 2, men and women relied on other members of their sex as mentors. What made women different was the fact that they empathized with other women in prison. Rita felt sorry for these women.

RITA: I'd say 60 percent of the women I knew in prison had a girlfriend. Women want it that way; they want someone to be with.

TRAMMELL: Are these good or bad relationships?

RITA: Mostly good. You get some of the hardcore women, some that have been in prison a while, they are tough girls and they will beat you up for sure if they think you deserve it. What happens is that some young girl gets to prison, you know the type, they've been through the system for a while and are beaten down pretty hard, and they are scared. These women end up with one of the bad-ass hard cases that offer to take care of them, get them extra food or watch their back from other women and stuff, and these young girls, they go with it cuz they're scared. I don't blame them; it's scary. Of course, this means these women own them.

TRAMMELL: Own them?

RITA: Yeah, almost like a slave or something. They boss them around, demand sex and stuff; it's weird. I didn't think women did this stuff to each other; I'd call it abuse. It doesn't happen too often, but it happens.

They explained that most relationships were mutually satisfactory, but some of the hard-core women controlled their girlfriends by offering them protection. Aura explained that some women seek out other women who will protect them:

Some women get a beat-down in prison, they get knocked around. I got knocked around pretty bad, so I get it. They are poor, no money for their canteen, get smacked around; sure, I get it, get with a big woman, a woman with money. Unless you've been in prison, you probably won't understand it. You see how these women turn into animals sometimes and so you hook up; I get it.

Others have documented the violence between incarcerated women (Alarid 2000; Greer 2000). However, there is no evidence that women are becoming more violent (Pollock and Davis 2005). Men are more likely to hurt or kill each other in prison (Harer and Langan 2001). I contend that violence is justified as a strategy of action, depending on the behavior of the victim.

Emily explained that women must have friends in prison in order to make it:

It's about survival, not sex or stuff. You hook up because you want to survive; you can't survive in prison alone. You get a huge target on your back if you are alone, and some get scared. They know they'll have to give it up sooner or later; that's a fact. You see, everyone is having sex in prison. You can say, "Hey, not me," but it'll happen; you can choose someone that is nice and stuff. You know, someone who will take care of you, give you money, or protect you from the really scary chicks.

Men described the victims of prison rape as culpable because they were weak. In other words, the norms of masculinity dictated that men remain tough; therefore, vulnerable men failed at being men. Women, however, contended that prison was tough on everyone and vulnerability did not mean failure.

Gender Roles and Violence

Most women had happy relationships in prison. However, when women talked about prison violence, they often explained that violent women acted like men. In other words, they assumed a masculine role in their relationships. Lauren told me that some women behaved like men and dominated their girlfriends: "The sex and shit, it was strange. These women really push each other around. I know this sounds bad but some women in prison, they're like men. They dress and act like men. I think they want to be the guy in the relationship. They completely control their girlfriends and God help them if they refuse to put out." Here, she told me that when women want to be the "guy" in the relationship, it meant controlling and dominating other women. It was particularly interesting to me how men and women described gender roles when telling me about these relationships. In both cases, the stronger person, male or female, was described in masculine terms. Olivia told me that prison relationships were so strange she "converted" to heterosexuality: "After seeing what women do to each other in prison, I went straight. Isn't that funny? I'd always been a lesbian, never liked men, but I turned in prison. After I got out, I got married, had kids, I like men now."

There were several interesting themes in their stories. Not all relationships were described in positive terms. Female inmates explained that some women controled each other and some used violence, and they described such women in masculine terms. In addition, Greer (2000) found that some women, called "canteen whores," took girlfriends who could offer them money or items from the prison store. Women in her study claimed that few of these prison relationships were based on actual love or companionship. Instead, they described how inmates use other inmates to get tangible items in prison.

The women I interviewed asserted that they behaved like men in order to control their girlfriends. Their attempts at domination affected the way they dressed and the level of violence they used. Some of these women also blamed the victim. Ella told me that women volunteered for relationships in prison and thus gave up their right to consent:

> Well, you should be able to say no. Of course you should; otherwise, it's rape. But women have to take some of the fault here. I see these young girls in college and stuff and they get wasted at some frat party or something and make out with all the guys and one or two of the guys takes her in a bedroom and has sex with her. Then she claims rape. You know, that's what wrong with women: they want the best of

both worlds. Same thing in prison: these young girls come in and want their mommy. They want someone to take care of them, but they know what that means. That means put out or shut up. Then they refuse and bad things happen. Well, jeez, sister, what the hell did you think was going to happen? There are no men outside that'll take that shit and neither will the dykes in prison. Part of me feels sorry for them, but part of me doesn't. They gotta take some blame here.

Molly complained that some women don't understand how prison relationship work:

> These women go into prison and think they are hot stuff. They had a lot of men outside, lots of boyfriends and shit. They get inside and pull the same shit, flirt with the big girls, ask for money or stuff, and they are cute so the girls are all over that. Well, this is prison; you can't say no in here. You can say no on the outside, cuz guys know you will call rape. On the inside, we don't snitch; you get what you get, and no one is coming to rescue you. I feel sorry for them; the popular girls learn that popularity is different in prison. It comes back to bite you on the ass.

Polly, a convicted prostitute, compared domineering women in prison to pimps who dominate their girlfriends:

> You know, some women get by on their looks, so they never have to learn to fight for anything. Then they get into prison, and they have no fucking clue about how to defend themselves or take care of themselves. A sugar daddy is one thing; you hook up with one of the scary dykes in prison and she's not going to baby you. She will tear you up and you can't say shit. They are more like a pimp or something; there's nothing you can do about it.

The women I interviewed in prison were separated from their families and children. They were humiliated and stigmatized by their prison experience, and they coped by taking drugs, finding a girlfriend, or isolating themselves. In this environment, a variety of sexual relationships were created, some of which were grounded in abuse. Most of the women explained that they simply went "gay for the stay," while others engaged in a type of protective pairing. In contrast to men, women in prison empathized with those who were abused. They understood how frightening prison could be, and they felt sorry for them. Women were allowed to be scared; they were allowed to seek help. They were given a certain amount of leeway to express weakness. Their situation was quite different from that of the men in my study, who distanced themselves from those who were sexually abused in prison. Also, some of these women blamed the victims for not keeping up their end of the bargain. In these narratives, we see that their argument is quite similar to that of their male counterparts. Inmates were deeply concerned about keeping their promises to one another in prison.

Conclusion

In recent years, scholars began focusing on sexual abuse between incarcerated women (Alarid 2000; Greer 2000). These studies found that some women sexually assault each other and not all prison relationships are friendly. By comparing the stories of men and women, I found some inmates in both men and women's prisons engage in what Donaldson (2001) would call protective pairing. Abused or scared inmates found someone to protect them and offered sex in return. These relationships could be violent, and the subordinated person lost power in exchange for this protection, but women mostly describe them as being like families.

Women are less violent than men, and it is reasonable to assume that prison rape is more of a problem in men's prisons. Violence and other interpersonal problems may have always been a problem for women, but they were overlooked or misclassified by prison officials or researchers because so many women were willing to discuss the benefits of these relationships.

Prison girlfriends seemed to love and care about each other. Their relationships appear to have been more functional than the arrangements in men's prisons. However, research now shows that some of these relationships have serious problems (Alarid 2000; Greer 2000). By comparing the stories told by men and women, we get a broader picture and see that some women abuse their girlfriends. We need not respond by discounting the benefits of these relationships, but we should be paying attention to the problems encountered in all romantic or sexual relationships. If women are willing to discuss sexual violence in prison, we should give them a voice to do so. We should also consider the fact that, for some men, prison relationships are not violent. It seems reasonable to assume that some men go "gay for the stay" and develop positive relationships with each other in prison.

Men described toughness and independence as the norms of prison masculinity. Their stories converged with those of women when they listed the benefits gained by trading sex for favors in prison. Of course, there is a continuum of inmate sexual behaviors. To be sure, there are consensual relationships in all prisons where no one is abused. As Fleisher and Kreinert (2009) point out, prison is a hypersexual environment with a variety of norms surrounding gender and sexuality. Those I interviewed seemed to be greatly concerned about the norms of reciprocation (Cialdini 1984). In prison, you cannot promise to do something and then back out. That is interpreted as a serious breach of norms, and those who breach that norm are deemed worthy of punishment. The difference between men and women is that women are more likely to feel sorry for the victim, whereas men despise those who are weak. Men who cannot perform their prescribed gender roles are targeted for abuse.

What does all of this say about rape, gender, and sex in prison? The official, quantitative reports on prison rape are hindered by the norms of prison culture. Researchers, lawmakers, and the general public may consider a wide variety of behaviors as sexual abuse, but inmates have a narrower view. Inmates' reluctance to label certain behaviors as rape will affect official numbers, and it may explain why prison rape is rarely reported. Rape may be a big problem in prison. However, the normative order dictates who is labeled a victim and who is labeled a rapist. In some cases, those dominating or abusing others are not completely blamed. The people I interviewed describe these arrangements as a consensual relationship. If there is abuse, the victims are described as partially or entirely to blame because they got something from the relationship. They may have been protected, or they may have received material goods. In either case, they gave up their right to say no.

What is interesting about these interviews is the way in which gender is discussed and organized in a same-sex environment. For the most part, gender norms are so internalized and institutionalized (Acker 1990; Bird and Sokolofski 2004; Britton 2003; Martin 2004) that both men and women used them without critically thinking about the behavior that takes place in these relationships. That makes sense: both men and women enter prison clearly understanding how men and women are supposed to act. They are then faced with the reality that there is a good deal of sex happening in prison. To explain this behavior, they draw from their ideas about gender, power, and inequality. What is especially interesting is how those exhibiting masculine traits are described as having more power. For both men and women, those who are weak are the losers. Although women often told me that they behaved better than men in prison, they also saw the value in being strong and capable.

Connell (1987, 2000) argued that gendered assumptions (male as strong, female as weak) strengthen male dominance in political and so-

cial life. He recommended that men become invested in gender equality by "undoing" gendered practices that subordinate women. However,
in separate studies Sharon R. Bird and Patricia Yancy Martin (Bird 2003;
Bird and Sokolofski 2004; Martin 2003, 2004) stated that men have no
vested interest in gender equality: "To undo gender, men not only have
to realize the harm created by engaging in masculinist practices, but
they have to become actively antimasculinist. This is a step that re-
quires men to stand in opposition to their own practices and the privileges those practices create, even though most men and many women
find such practices quite acceptable, normal, and desirable" (Bird 2003:
368). Here, Bird explained that undoing gender is a costly behavior for
men, who lose patriarchal power by doing so. In other words, practicing (or doing) gender benefits men more than women. My data show
Bird is correct on two accounts. First, men in prison describe doing
gender in a way that feminizes men. They discussed these behaviors in
a way that always posited the "female" as weak and deviant. Clearly,
the norms of protective pairing are constructed in a way that maintains
patriarchal power for the majority of men in prison occupying the
"male" role.

Second, Bird is correct that "most men and many women find such
practices quite acceptable, normal, and desirable" (368). The women in
my study also did gender in a way that highlighted male domination.
Gender is so internalized and institutionalized that both men and women
recreated the norms of gender inequality, even though they were in a
same-sex environment. To be sure, women take a softer approach to
these norms, and some identify with the victim. However, my case study
shows the power of hegemonic masculinity. It is not simply that men
dominate women; instead, women buy into their own oppression. Their
acceptance of norms that harm them affects prison culture because inmates learn to control others as part of a gendered arrangement that is
familiar to them. Remember, it is the performance that is important
(Sampson and Bean 2006). Therefore, inmates "perform" for other inmates, and culture develops through this interactive process.

Researchers have detailed how men adhere to prescribed gender
norms more rigidly than women (Bourdieu 2001; McGuffey and Rich
1999; Pollack 1999; Thorne 1993, 1998). Women and girls have some
leeway to be "tomboys" or androgynous, but effeminate boys or men
"failed at being men" (Thorne 1993:116). Although women entering
into an all-male environment (the firehouse or the military) will not necessarily be accepted, gender is a bit more flexible for women. Among

women in prison, the masculine inmate controls her girlfriend because she is the "man" in the relationship and provides protection for her partner. In this book, I highlight how effeminate men fail at masculinity and masculine women succeed in controlling others. In other words, having masculine traits is somewhat advantageous for both men and women living in prison.

5

Interpersonal Conflict

In this chapter, I explore how men and women describe conflict and conflict resolution. Specifically, I let interviewees describe daily problems that may or may not result in violence. Early sociological research described prisons as hierarchical communities in which authority reigned from the top down and cooperation was the key to social order (Cloward 1960; Goffman 1961; Sykes 1958). Prisoners created an inmate code consisting of norms and rules about inmate conduct. In doing so, they attempted to standardize inmate culture. Cons, or solid cons, learned and promoted the code, while inmates simply did their time and parole (Terry 1997; Trammell 2009b). To some extent, these norms dictated how inmates behaved and solved problems. In other words, inmates usually did not have a functional working relationship with prison staff; they probably handled many of their own problems.

Conflict is a part of our daily lives. In prison, it is especially hard to avoid some problems because of the closed environment. Also, inmates have little power; they are limited in how they can respond to conflict. Of course, some inmates report violence to the staff, and some will work with them to solve interpersonal problems. However, for most inmates, there is a lot of pressure to keep the prison staff at bay.

In 2006, the Commission on Safety and Abuse in America's Prisons released a report focusing on the current state of US prisons. In its report, the commission recommended that prison officials in the United States promote an ongoing "culture of mutual respect" and "create a positive culture in jails and prisons grounded in an ethic of respectful behavior and interpersonal communication that benefits prisoners and staff" (Gibbons and Katzenbach 2006:75). The commission interviewed correctional staff, inmates, and national experts to evaluate the current state of US prisons. Also, the commission held open hearings, which allowed people to publicly discuss important issues such as overcrowded prisons, violence, rehabilitation, and prison culture.

The report outlined several recommendations to reduce these problems. For example, it recommended that US prisons reduce inmate overcrowding and minimize the time inmates spend in isolation/segregation. It also suggested that Americans pay close attention to how conflict is managed in prison. If the goal is to rehabilitate offenders and prepare them for release, then officials should have a better understanding of what inmates learn in prison. It is possible to improve prison culture and make prisons safe and productive instruments of change (Gibbons and Katzenbach 2006).

In this chapter, I focus on how inmates describe the daily problems of prison life and how conflict sometimes leads to violence. I hope this chapter will add to the national discussion about prison culture and conflict management.

Conflict and Violence

The men in my study explained that the causes of violence are usually disrespect, drugs, theft, and race. They often fought with their roommates, whom they called their "cellie." As discussed in Chapter 3, men refused to share a cell with a man of another race. However, there were still problems between cellies. All the men in my study told me that they had fights or disagreements with them. Some of these problems happened because their cellie took their things. Sometimes, these men simply annoyed them.

Seth talked about how he had to beat up his cellie: "My cellie and I got into it once; he was a Peckerwood asshole. He was really dumb. He used to tell me these dumb stories, and he really got on my nerves. I finally had enough, and I gave him a beat-down. He would just not shut up. All I wanted him to do was shut up. If he shut up, I wouldn't have to do it. God, he pissed me off." Violence was sometimes used to teach someone a lesson about manners. In Seth's case, the problem was compounded by the fact that he had to live with this man. His cellie did not do anything specific like steal from him or hurt him; it was simply a personality conflict that resulted in violence. Other men discussed what happens when men refused to follow basic social rules. Luke told me that his cellie would not shower:

He was in for a month or so and he wouldn't shower, and I mean he stunk like you would not believe. You cannot imagine what a man smells like after that time. I go talk with the guy and ask him what the deal is. He said that he didn't want to shower with a bunch of dudes. I told him that he needed to shower, or I'd beat him up. Trust me, there was a line of guys ready to beat him up over this. He says that he'll take his chances. The next day, I beat his smelly ass like it's never been beat before. He took a shower after that. In fact, he told me later that he appreciated me helping him out. He did okay after that.

Geraldo had problems with his cellmate, who wouldn't leave his things alone: "I got into it with my cellie; I hated the guy so much. He touched my stuff and I think he was gay. I had to beat him up a few times before he requested a transfer. I got a great guy after that; we're still friends. He knew to leave my shit alone and showed respect." In these cases, Geraldo and Luke were not threatened by their cellie, nor did they have any serious problems with them. Instead, conflict resulted from the daily annoyances of having to live with a roommate.

Ronald described the difficulties of getting along with other people in prison:

> You just get frustrated; you have bad days just like everyone else. If you are in a bad mood outside of prison, you just go have a beer, hang out with your boys. In prison you end up taking it out on someone. I remember having a bad attitude one time and the cop asks what the problem is. I tell him that I'm in a pissy mood; I feel like beating down a baby killer or something, you know, just beat someone down. He just laughed. I ended up getting into it with my cellie. He just looked at me wrong, and I let him have it. We punched each other for a few minutes.

All these men were forced to live in very small cells with men they had never met before. They refused to share a cell with men of another race, but that only helped them maintain their standing in their gang; it did not guarantee that they would like their cellmates. Outside prison, they could move out or find someone else to live with. In prison, they were stuck with few options. In some cases, violence was used to control others and relieve the pressure. Kory told me this story:

> I had a few problems with the guys I bunked with. I'll be cool for a while but when you've had enough, you have to step up and do something about it. I got transferred like three times for fighting, and it's usually stuff in the cell. One guy, he was a real cock. He took my stuff and shot his mouth off. No one could stand this guy. I actually think

that the guards put him with me cuz they knew I'd kick his ass. I finally had it, and I beat him up. I guess I really hurt him cuz the next thing I know, he's in the infirmary and I'm transferring out. They don't like to keep people around if they fight too much, so I had to leave. It was fine by me.

Kory's story interested me for several reasons. First, men who fight are often transferred to another cell or another prison. Men were quick to point to this as one way to deal with problem cellies. They beat them up and the cellie could request to go to the protective custody yard, or one of them changed cells. For men, it was one (albeit extreme) way to get what they wanted, but they told me that this strategy worked. Second, Kory stated that this man annoyed everyone, including correctional officers, so he believes that they intentionally paired him with this person. In other words, they shared responsibility for the fight. There is no way to determine if what Kory said is true. However, these men definitely believed that their frustration was universal and that they were justified in committing violence because everyone had a problem with annoying inmates. Therefore, violence solved a universal problem.

Tyler explained how violence was also used to make others respect you:

> TYLER: I got into a fight with this guy; he owed me money. I told his boys that they need to talk with him and they were like, "What can we do about it?" which means that I gotta go get the money myself. I go talk with him, and he spits on me. What the hell? I wasn't going to beat him up, but now I have to on principle alone. I grabbed him and got him in a headlock, tried to choke him out. He got away, but I think he was dizzy and I punched him around for maybe a minute or so. What a dumbass. If he was cool, nothing would happen. Instead, he has to be a total dick and spit at me. Who does that? What are we, ten years old?
>
> TRAMMELL: Did you get your money?
>
> TYLER: Hell, yeah, I got my money. I will always get my money. Also, he learned some manners. I think that, for some of these guys, they just don't know how to act; they have no class. I knew plenty of guys who had no education and their parents did a shitty job with them. It's just a matter of how they were raised.

Originally, Tyler had a conflict with another inmate about a drug debt, which escalated because the man handled the situation badly. Men who did not show respect were basically challenging others to fight. Vincent also had a problem with his cellie. He believed that he had to fight his cellie in order to control him. "I waited for my cellie to come back and I jumped him, punched him in the ribs a few times then I stuck his head in the toilet. He learned some respect after that. If you give them an inch, they'll take a foot. You have to establish the ranking right away, or these guys will walk all over you." Pedro told a similar story:

> I would have food in my cell, and my cellie would eat it. I ignored it the first time, but after that I had to show him that I'm not messing around. I'm not a punk. In the joint, all you have is yourself and your honor. I waited for him to come back to the cell and I asked him about my food, and he just looked at me. I threw a punch and he went down. He never even said anything. He never touched my food again.

To be sure, these men were establishing their place in the social hierarchy. What is interesting is that men who acted out or annoyed others were sometimes pushed to the bottom of the pecking order. In other words, those who do not behave in a respectful manner must be taught a lesson. They also needed to be taken down a peg or two. What was common to all these stories was that violence solved their problems. For example, Miguel told me how he held his own in a dominance fight:

> My cellie attacked me once and we went at it pretty bad; it felt like an hour, but it was probably about ten minutes. This guy was a border brother and wanted to show me how tough he is. I ran with the Southerners, so I can't take that from him, I had to fight back and take him down. In truth, it was probably a draw, but he never pulled that shit with me again; he learned to leave me alone and shit.

Roman also attacked a fellow gang member who aggravated him: "He was just being a dick. I don't even remember what he said to me, but you know how some people just piss you off? It was like that; he used to joke about my hair and shit, just aggravate me, you know? I finally had it, and I took him in a blind spot and popped him once in the mouth. That's all it took, one punch and he went down. He wasn't so mouthy after that."

These men used violence instrumentally to show others that they were in charge. They were in prison, but they did not have to tolerate the bad behavior of fellow inmates. All the men in my study described beating up men who had it coming because they were annoying. These conflicts had nothing to do with a tangible threat or gang initiation. They involved dealing with daily problems that happen in all social settings. The men explained how their victims pushed their buttons or overstepped their boundaries. If they lived outside prison, they could avoid each other. In order to put the annoying people back in their place, violence was performed. It was a type of corporal punishment doled out to stop or prevent the bad behavior of others. It also helps the aggressors maintain their own performances as tough and authoritative men.

Inmates described being frustrated by conflicts with their cellmates. Some of this frustration came from their lack of formal options. Several men told me how they would have handled things differently in another social setting. For example, Ronald explained that he would go out and have a beer with his friends. However, in prison, they did not make the official rules. They could not handpick their cellmates, and they could not leave the prison. They knew they could not go through formal channels to deal with these daily annoyances. Also, these prisons were all overcrowded. Overcrowding would make these problems especially unbearable as more and more people entered prison.

Culturally, inmates cannot work with prison staff, and they must act tough because of the norms laid down by the inmate code (Sykes 1958; Terry 1997; Trammell 2009b). Therefore, prison culture shaped their behavior and their performances. They had to show others that they were worthy of respect. To a large extent, culture is shaped by the daily interaction between people (Sampson and Bean 2006; Stowell and Byrne 2008; Swidler 1986). Through this interactive process, men learned the pecking order quickly. Those who challenged them must be dealt with accordingly. These rules normalized violence as a coping strategy in prison. In other words, strength became synonymous with violence.

Obviously, public performance is important in maintaining a worthy identity (Stowell and Byrne 2008). The fact that men used violence for such mundane problems indicates that violence is perfectly acceptable in this social setting. If they beat down another inmate, they projected an image of strength and authority. Of course, they had other options. They could have ignored obnoxious inmates or talked through their problems. Instead, these men decided to use violence as a quick solution.

The Pains of Incarceration

Men described conflict with correctional officers and other prison staff, which could also lead to violence. However, male inmates were reluctant to fight prison staff. They were concerned about retaliation and prison lockdowns. Chuck told me a poignant story about a lockdown:

> They were already on lockdown when I went in, so the lockdown lasted
> for eleven months total. You end up panicking sometimes cuz I needed
> my insulin and I was locked down in my cell and the cops would for-
> get to bring me my stuff and I'd pass out. If I was able to move around,
> I could have told someone, but you don't see anyone all damn day. By
> the time they get to me, I'm passed out from not getting my meds. It's
> like, oops, sorry, dude, we forgot you again. I always wondered what
> the hell they were doing. If everyone is locked down, they don't have
> much to do, right? Why can't they remember my meds?

Chuck originally told me that he experienced no problems with correctional officers but then told me this story. He was bothered by the fact
that they were neglecting him, but he did not interpret their behavior as
a direct threat or interpersonal conflict. Daniel, however, told me about
a different experience: "The guards will mess with you, and they will be
jerks. There were some that I just hated. This one guy would say shit to
me every day, every damned day. I would roll my eyes and ignore him
and he just got worse. Eventually he got the hint and ignored me too."

Inmates know that assaulting prison staff will cause them serious
problems, including a formal reprimand. It will be reported, which means
that they will go to administrative segregation (commonly called ad seg,
or the hole), a one-person cell where inmates are held after they fight. It
is standard procedure to send all offending parties to these solitary confinement cells in order to calm them down or to punish them. Also, inmates believe that the staff will retaliate, which could make their lives
miserable. Assaulting prison staff seriously damages the relationship between inmates and staff that is vital to rehabilitation.

James explained that prison staff was mostly unable to resolve
conflict:

> I got jumped one time. I didn't even see the guy who hit me from be-
> hind, I get hit and fall to my knees and I get written up for mutual com-
> bat. I get hit in the back of my head; how is that mutual? They say they
> caught the guy and that it was a "black thing." What the hell does that
> mean? I get hit, they claim it's about race, and I get the 115. Those
> guys are incompetent and they have no sympathy for victims.

Leon stated that the prison staff often made their daily problems worse:

> The worst part about prison is the food. It is unbelievably bad. I lost so
> much weight because I could not eat that crap. It's just stressful. This
> one day, I wasn't feeling well; I think I got a cold. We get no medi-
> cine; if you ask for something for your cold, they'll give you some
> Tylenol. So I'm sick and the food is really bad, so I don't eat cuz the
> food is bad, and I go to my work detail and I'm worn out. The cops are

standing around while we're working, just talking smack to us. What the hell? It's all I can do to not smack one in the mouth. They wonder why we fight and why we're always so angry. If they didn't say shit to us, like, all the time, we'd probably get along. What the hell?

Although the inmate code prevented inmates from working with staff, it appears that staff also contributed to the problem. Their actions might not result in assaults against them, but they could instigate violence. Adam told me this story: "They called me 'trailer-park' cuz I guess they think I'm white trash. They also saw my brand; they see that I'm a skinhead, so I'm white trash. They should know. Those assholes looked like they came right out of the park, but they call me that shit. Okay, whatever, I'll end up beating someone up, and you'll have to clean it up, so go ahead, piss me off."

Like Adam, Martino told me that they would intentionally make more work for the staff. "Some of the guys are okay; they don't say anything to you and they don't start shit. Other guys act like they are about twelve years old. They aggravate you and throw their weight around. Some of the older guys figured it out. If they just show respect then it makes their job easier. If they piss me off and I end up punching someone out, they have to break up a fight." In other words, male inmates got even with the staff indirectly. They believed their method worked because it inconvenienced the staff, and they got away with it because their fellow inmates refused to snitch on them.

If the staff was rude or antagonistic, it drove a wedge between these two groups, as Carlos stated:

> Those guys are fucking useless. Why would I ever go to them with my problems? They are always standing around, doing nothing, or they say shit to us to piss us off. Look, I don't know how much they make, but it's too much. If some guy is hassling me, I'm supposed to go the guards? No, I'd go to my boys or take care of the situation myself. Those guys are not problem solvers, you know.

Several men made similar claims. They believed that it was easier to handle problems themselves than to work with the prison staff. Hal had this to say:

> HAL: Why on earth would I go to them? First of all, they don't give a shit, and you can complain all you want and nothing will get done. Secondly, they will make things worse because the men will be pissed that you ran to the cops for help. Those guys do nothing but stand around waiting for their shift to end and give us grief. It's re-

ally not worth it. Why would I put myself at risk and give them anything? They get information and use it against us.

TRAMMELL: What do you mean?

HAL: They found out that this new guy was giving head to anther guy.
He was probably getting drugs or something for it, who knows? The
cops made fun of the guy and he tried to kill himself. This is what
I mean; if the people in charge don't give a shit, they'll make it
worse on you. I heard they were only pissed because they had to
fill out paperwork on the guy. Never mind that they helped cause
this problem.

Interpersonal conflict with correctional officers differs from the conflict with fellow inmates. No one in my study described violence directed
at the prison staff. Instead, several men explained that correctional officers would make them angry, and then they took it out on each other.
Fighting with a fellow inmate was a way to get even. Violence, as a strategy, was an aggressive way to maintain your position in the pecking order
and make more work for prison staff. Again, this reasoning normalized
violence as a coping mechanism.

Women's Fights in Prison

The women in my study did not fight like the men. They told me that
women in prison might fight, but they were quick to tell me that no one
wanted to seriously hurt each other. This was interesting, considering
the serious acts of violence they described. The fights often involved
slapping, hitting, pulling hair, and kicking. Also, they told me they
yelled at one another, but that did not usually end in physical violence.
Lucy described a typical fight between women: "It's more about cat-
fights and throwing words around. They yell back and forth at each
other. Not a lot of violence, no stabbings. The worst you're going to get
probably is punching, fist to fist. Hand combat. You don't see women
making shanks." All the women I interviewed had verbal fights in
prison, and 61 percent admitted to hitting or slapping other women. Yet
Rita, like other women, always stated that no one was hurt: "Women
fight but not serious stuff; we didn't ever want to really, you know, hurt
each other or kill each other. We never wanted to do serious damage.
Women will scar each other and stuff, leave someone's face scarred but
not kill or stab each other; you'd need to talk to the men about that
stuff." Charlotte agreed that most fights were minor: "We didn't fight
much, some slaps here and there, mostly over taking my stuff, but jeez,

I would never hurt someone." Julia went so far as to claim that she was squeamish and so she avoided fistfights: "I fought with a woman once; we punched each other, maybe for a few minutes. I lost a tooth over it, but I don't think she was hurt. Mostly bruises, nothing serious. I'm pretty squeamish about blood and stuff and so I couldn't really throw down like the guys do, stabbing each other and stuff, that's amazing." A key difference between men's and women's violence is that women never admitted that they wanted to kill someone. Men often used violence to achieve some goal, whereas women described only sporadic fights.

In Chapter 4, I reported how women complained that they did not get the same privileges as men because they were less violent. Men used violence if they believed it would solve a problem, but women like Ella discussed the fact that they were unwilling to fight. "We're not like the men. They rape each other cuz they want to control each other and they want to make someone the woman. They want control. Women do not do this. We are not taught to do this." Olivia claimed that women in prison never wanted to control other women. "I know a few guys who went to prison. They beat each other up at the drop of a hat. They like to have power over each other. We were very different. Lots of time, we worked together and everyone had friends. There just isn't a big problem with violence in our prisons." Caroline agreed, more or less: "I got into a few fights in prison, but no one was hurt and we mostly just pulled hair and stuff. There was a lot of yelling. There were a lot of women who scared me, but I never thought they'd kill me. I could tell someone off and nothing much would happen."

At the heart of Olivia's argument is her lack of interest in controlling others in prison. Caroline also stated that using violence as a mechanism of control is unnecessary because women are easy to get along with. Throughout this book, I have given examples of the problems women faced in prison. They did not necessarily like their cellmates, they did not like being told what to do, or they had to deal with problem inmates. At the same time, they were not willing to put shot-callers in charge or use lethal violence. When asked why, they stated that they were not "taught" to fight, which is somewhat true.

Throughout our lives, most of us are socialized to conform to our prescribed gender roles. Men are taught to compete, whereas women are taught to cooperate. One difference between the men and women quoted in this book is that women are not really equipped to use violence as a tool. Of course, the majority of the women I interviewed (61 percent) fought in prison. Upon reflection, they described these events as brief and unproblematic. The meaning behind their actions differs from that of their male counterparts, who often describe violence as a way to gain control. Women realized that their fights challenged prescribed gender norms, so they made sure to tell me that they never really hurt anyone.

They told me that their unwillingness to fight resulted in another layer of victimization. They were not "taught" to fight, which meant that they had less control in prison. They were "told what to do," which meant that they had no power. Their frustration and loss of power often led to negatives attitudes about the state and the criminal justice system, such as that expressed by Prudence: "Women get screwed in every aspect of the system. We do the right thing: we don't fight back because that's what we're trained to do, and what's our reward? The system was made by and set up for men, not us. Otherwise we would be taught to fight back, to not take the shit they throw at us." From their perspective, the criminal justice system rewarded men for their violence. Lupe felt bitter that men got so much care in prison:

> You know, the men get so much more. They get programs and therapy cuz they are violent offenders. We go in for drugs, and they rape women. They get therapy cuz the government worries about them. The government has to know where they are and shit. Maybe we should hurt people too. Maybe that's what it'll take to get the government to see we need help too. Instead, we only shoot up drugs, so we're not a real threat. You know, they have this war on drugs because drugs are our big problem. Then they ignore drug addicts and reward the pervert rapists who really hurt people.

Ella agreed, saying: "Women don't get any programs cuz they have to take care of the real violent offenders. We deal drugs, you know, cuz our boyfriends deal drugs, so we deal with them and we don't murder or rape people, so we don't deserve any kind of program. It's kind of, excuse my language, fucked up. I should not have to hurt people to get treatment." Barbara made a similar claim: "If they really cared about women, they would give us programs. They would not make us wait. I talked with guys who said that there were tons of things for them in prison, but they didn't want them. We scream for these things and get nothing. I think it's sexism."

Lupe and Ella noted that violent offenders or sex offenders are given special services to control or cure them. To be sure, there are services for sex offenders because the courts often mandate treatment. The goal is to reduce their chances of re-offending once they leave prison. Simply put, if a sex offender commits more crimes, people get hurt. Yet some women in prison believed that rehabilitative services rewarded sex offenders.

Barbara interpreted the plethora of services for men and the lack of services for women as a serious problem for women who are, quite frankly, less likely to be violent. Her attitude went beyond the idea that the squeaky wheel gets the oil. Instead, she, like other women I interviewed, claimed that the criminal justice system rewarded men for being violent and for committing sexual assault. Marilyn seconded her opinion: "Women are not willing to hurt each other; we don't hurt each other in prison. Instead we get the lousy food, too many people in our cells and they get what they want. When we leave prison, we are homeless, have no money and employers treat us like trash so we get no jobs." Joanne also blamed the sex offenders for getting services that could be devoted to women's needs: "I kept asking for substance abuse counseling and they kept telling me that they don't have enough money to put everyone in rehab. Of course, the sex offenders get everything they want. They save all of the money for the men because they are a bigger threat. I don't scare anyone so I was put on a waiting list for services. I never got shit."

Of course, women still have options for solving daily problems. However, since violence is not a viable choice, they must find other ways to deal with interpersonal conflict in prison.

Nonviolent Solutions

Most women talked about how they solved their problems without using violence. They sometimes avoided problem inmates, although that was not always possible. When they did deal with these women, some used rumors or gossip as a weapon. Rosario told me this story:

> Women who are younger may fight more, you know, use their fists, but mostly women just tell each other off. They will have their friends back each other up and will confront each other. I had a woman who was a complete bitch; I told her friends that she talked about them, which was true. You should have heard what she said. I told her friends that she spreads rumors and stuff, and they left her alone after that. That's about the worst of it.

Karla ignored her cellie when she got angry: "My cellie yelled at me once cuz she thought I took her stuff; I just ignored her. She was only interested in getting attention. If you ignored her, it drove her nuts. She would yell about something, and I'd give her the silent treatment and pretty soon, she was acting like an adult again." Bella explained that women learn how to avoid violence: "Guys always say that they can't understand what we want. If you know women, you know how to avoid problems. I got into plenty of fights in prison, but I also avoided fights. I only fought if someone attacked me. There's no need to start shit if you don't have to. That's the problem with men. They all want to control each other."

These women avoided violence by focusing on the weaknesses of their fellow inmates. The fact that their friends and cellies changed their behavior indicates that this strategy sometimes works. It also means that women do control each other. Despite the fact that they claim to avoid problems by not controlling each other, they shaped the behavior of others by focusing on the things women value. The men quoted in this book valued strength. The women, in their own way, knew exactly what to do to make other women fall in line.

Their strategy could be called relational aggression (Trammell 2009a:268), which is defined as "a form of emotional and psychological violence used to ruin relationships and sever social ties." Although female inmates specifically targeted relationships, they avoided physical violence and denounced it as unfeminine. According to official incident reports, women commit an average of 304 documented assaults each year, whereas men carry out an average of 6,684 assaults in California prisons (California Department of Corrections and Rehabilitation 2006a). However, women can, and do, hurt each other in prison (Alarid 2000; Greer 2000; Trammell 2009a). The women I interviewed seemed to be ashamed of it and were less likely to brag about their fights.

Just like their male counterparts, women also refused to ask prison staff for help with their problems. Marilyn told me this story:

MARILYN: I had a woman hit me once. What could I do? Nothing, really. I knew a few of her friends, and they told me that she was just being a bitch. She didn't hurt me or anything.

TRAMMELL: Did you report it?

MARILYN: No, of course not. If I got stabbed or something, that's different. Look, that's what women do, we try to control each other and we get frustrated, so yeah, someone gets hit. We handled it fine. I think her friends saw that she's a bitch and they know she was wrong, so she learned to behave herself.

Some women discussed the "code of silence," which prohibits inmates from working with staff. In fact, Hayley stated that the prison staff encourage this agreement:

There is a code of silence about issues. The cops tell us not to complain, not to report stuff because they don't want to do work. They don't want to fill out paperwork and investigate a problem. I told one of them once that my cellie was insane, and they said that I should deal with it. Isn't that their job? Why should I deal with their problem? I have to deal with a big load of shit because they don't want to.

I asked female inmates if they ever complained about these issues, and most women said that they had, at one time or another, used the formal CDCR 602 grievance procedure but nothing happened. For example, Molly told me: "We can file a 602, but they ignore those, and instead, they tell us that we can't talk to anyone about these things. It's not like it's just some guard that does this; they are the government. It's the same group of men that take control of our lives." Olivia told me how difficult it was to get medical care in prison:

I was an IV drug user going in, and when you're an IV user, you end up sharing needles. Knowing you share stuff and Hepatitis C. I kept telling them that I wanted to be tested. I ended up with Hep C and they didn't diagnose it until I got really sick, jaundice and fevers and stuff. I was really sick. I lost $16,000 worth of teeth because all they do is extractions. I came out without teeth. I went in a beautiful girl and came out a beautiful toothless girl. I had to turn in so many 602s to get treatment for my medical condition. I finally got it, but the medical is so awful if you don't have any money. I know of three women that died in prison because of HIV. If they have HIV, sometimes they get some treatment but they come out much sicker than when you went in.

Alexandria implicated the corrections system overall: "You don't understand, it's the whole system, I turned in lots of 602s and they lost or ignored them; I never received any response. What are they going to do, anyway? These men control us; it's their system. It's the way it is. We are a number to them; we're not even human." Karla told me this story about losing her sons while in prison:

I was in prison a month and my two teenage sons were murdered. I put in a request for a temporary leave to attend their funerals, which under Title 15 (California Code of Regulations: Title 15, Crime Prevention and Corrections) I'm entitled to. It was approved and the day before the funeral, I was taken to the reception area of prison and left there for twenty-one hours. They forgot about me. When they realized I was there, someone came and got me and took me back to my cell. I missed the funerals. Now here's the deal. They broke their own code by not letting me go, they broke another code by leaving me in the reception area for so long, and they broke the "cruel and unusual" code for making me miss my sons' funerals. I filed the 602 a year and a half ago, and

I never heard anything. I should sue them; I know I'd win. I'm telling you, they throw those things out.

Women were more likely than men to file complaints, and all but one claimed that she got a response. She told me that they responded by telling her that there was nothing they could do about her problem. If these stories are true, they build another wall between the inmates and prison staff. They also explain why interviewees stated that they refused to ask for help from the prison staff. Stephanie's opinion was typical: "If someone is just driving me crazy, I'm not reporting that. That's something I can deal with. I'm a grown woman and I think I can deal with a problem child, you know?"

Owen (1998:168) explained that many women became "prison-smart" in order to survive the pains of incarceration:

> Through past incarcerations, continuing contact with the criminal justice system, and a commitment to knowing "what is happening," the prison-smart woman negotiates the prison world on her own terms. The prison-smart woman can turn this specialized knowledge to her advantage, cultivating relationships with both staff and other prisoners that allow her some measure of freedom and autonomy in her everyday life, operating narrowly within the prison's rules and regulations.

Prison-smart women are usually lifers or women serving long sentences who, after going through a rough adjustment period, stay out of trouble and cultivate a daily routine devoid of conflict. Other women may come to these women, asking for advice about their daily problems. I interviewed several older women who fit this profile, such as Charlotte:

> The girls would come to me for advice. I managed a business outside of prison, and I'm a lot older than most of the girls inside. If you're older, like me, people mostly leave you alone, and you don't have a lot of problems. I remember these two girls came to me once asking about work duty. I told them to work hard and get their work done. If you are lazy, they won't work with you to switch to a better job, you know? It's about strategy; it's about working smart. I would tell them about my job outside and how I had to manage the workers and that hard work impressed me. Also, if you are working hard, you stay out of trouble, right? If you are doing your job, cleaning your cell, going to church and stuff, you don't have time to do drugs or pick fights.

Emma said that she learned to let things go as she got older:

> I used to fight a lot when I was younger, that's for sure. But you know what? You grow up and you learn that nothing is worth it. I remember

this young girl, maybe twenty-four or twenty-five years old, she called me a bitch. If she said that to me when I was young, I would have taken her down. I just looked at her and said, "Girl, you won't last long with that attitude; stop fighting and start working on yourself." She never bothered me again and I think she learned something about real power. You can beat someone down and you can hurt others with words or you can get real power by living clean and making something of yourself.

As Owen (1998) pointed out, age and experience helped some women stay out of trouble and possibly assist other inmates. Neither of these women were serving life sentences, but Charlotte was in for six years, and both of them had jobs and real world experience outside prison. This, along with their age, made them stand out as smart and experienced. Even more important, other women listened to them about working hard and improving their lives. In a similar vein, Lauren used her experience in prison to help female parolees:

> I know what these women go through, and I know what they need. I tried to help girls in prison, and I started working in a program when I got out. I started bringing in the girls who were leaving and I would help them get their licenses back and I would get them to [an Alcoholics Anonymous] meeting or help them fill out a job application. You know what? You can't apply for a job at a grocery story without using a computer; it's all online now. If you don't know computers, you can't get a job. I got some local businesses to donate money to get us some computers, and I found a used van to take the girls around in. Why isn't anyone else doing this? I'm doing it because I know what's up.

Stella told me the same story from the younger women's side: "I was so lost when I went to prison. I was lucky; I met a woman who was incredibly smart, and she told me what to do and who to trust. She was our go-to person, you know? She was one of those women who just knew everything and was always right. She'd been in prison for a long time and really knew the ropes. I think we would be lost without her." Several women talked about "giving back" to their community and helping one another. These women also explained that doing these things made your own life easier in prison because you focus on positive things rather than drugs or fighting. By mentoring others, women gained the confidence to reach out to local businesses for help. That helped them maintain a worthy identity as a successful person who is determined to stay out of prison.

Many times, women who commit crimes or violence are labeled as crazy or sick (Stanko 2001). While men told me stories about putting others in their place and beating up obnoxious inmates, women tried to cling to their assigned gender roles and mother other inmates. They had already breached the norms of female behavior by being arrested and incarcerated. Denouncing violence was one way they could reduce their own stigma. Mentoring others or helping parolees also helped them overcome the shame of being an ex-convict.

Women often talked about the violence in men's prisons. I believe that they used it as a reference point, to show me that women are different. None of the women I interviewed admitted to stabbing or trying to kill another woman. That group included women who were convicted of attempted murder, robbery, domestic violence, and assault and battery. For the most part, they avoided prison violence by finding other ways to deal with problems.

Men, however, described a prison hierarchy where the tough survive. They sometimes dealt with their daily problems by using violence. This certainly does not mean that men solved every problem with a fight. Nor does it mean that men never talk through their problems or find other ways to resolve conflict. However, 95 percent of the men in my study had at least one fight in prison.

Conclusion

Former inmates outlined some of the daily problems that all of them dealt with in prison. Anyone who has lived or worked with others has dealt with people who aggravated them. There are norms about resolving conflict with these people in all social settings. In prison, formal options are limited because prisoners cannot leave and have little power over where they sleep and keep their things. They live in overcrowded cells in overcrowded prisons and have almost no privacy. For them, daily problems are more salient. The intense nature of prison life certainly does not excuse the use of violence, but it puts it in context.

If inmates wished to pursue formal solutions to conflict, they could ask for a new cellmate or report problem behavior to prison staff. Instead, they handled these problems by adhering to the code of silence in prison, which meant that they took care of their own problems. To a large degree, their choice of action was based on the expectations of prison culture. In prison, it is important to work outside formal channels, which shapes how inmates choose their tactics: men pushed each other around, and women tried to outsmart each other. Older, more experienced women used their status to avoid trouble and help others. They also described how they maintained cultural norms about conflict and conflict resolution. Men and women clearly understood what their fellow inmates valued (for men, strength and respect; for women, friendships and attention), and this influenced their performances.

Although women sometimes used violence, they stated that they never hurt each other and downplayed the impact of physical violence. They did not want the stigma associated with violent action to be attached to them. At the same time, men showed how violence was used instrumentally to put others in their place. They have absolutely no problem with others thinking they are violent as long as there is a valid reason for such behavior. In both cases, men and women described the performance of controlled and capable inmates who settled their own problems without the help of the prison staff.

6

Mechanisms
of Social Control

For the most part, people conform to the norms of their society. However, under certain circumstances, we all deviate from those norms. We break rules, and in some cases, we even break the law. At the time I collected my data, inmates were given a California Code of Regulations, Title 15, handbook when they entered prison. They were told to read and follow the rules outlined in the handbook. They faced formal sanctions if they were caught breaking those rules. As I have pointed out in the previous chapters, inmates create informal norms and make sure that new inmates understand and follow these norms. In this chapter, I focus on formal and informal mechanisms of social control in prison. In doing so, I pay particular attention to how interviewees described skirting the formal rules.

The California Department of Corrections and Rehabilitation responds to rule infractions by giving the inmate a CDCR 115 violation (see Table 6.1). There are two types of infractions: serious (threatening to safety or security such as assaults or escape) or administrative (hiding food, destroying state property). Serious 115 violations result in a loss of "good time" release credit for the inmate (California Department of Corrections and Rehabilitation 2003). However, my interviewees told me that if they went ninety days without another 115, they should gain that credit back. If they were caught fighting, they were sent to the administrative segregation unit (the hole, or ad seg). However, that was usually temporary. Furthermore, if they were unable to stop fighting with other inmates or were threatened, they could be transferred to another prison. In fact, several men told me that they had to be transferred because of fighting.

I asked the men in my study to describe the different types of violence they experienced or witnessed in prison. Using their terms, I cre-

Table 6.1 Formal Response to Rule Violation

Rule Violation Report (CDCR Form 115)
Official written report on rule violations that may be used to reduce or eliminate good time credit.

Administrative 115 Report
Violation involves a nonviolent or nonthreatening rule violation such as misuse of food or misuse of phone privileges.

Serious 115 Report
Violation involves a threat to security or violent action, such as use of force or violence, or serious disruption of facility operations.

Inmate Lockdown
A section of the prison is closed, or locked down, services are suspended, inmates are confined to cells, and inmates who are escorted to their work detail perform only critical work duties. The administration decides the parameters of the lockdown and returns to normal operations when the threat to security is eliminated.

Administrative Segregation Unit
If inmates receive serious 115 reports and/or are a threat to institutional order, they are sent to the "hole," or solitary confinement. Victims of violence are also put into administrative segregation (ASU, "ad seg") for their own protection. This is a separate housing unit apart from the general housing areas.

Confinement to Quarters (CTQ)
Inmates are confined to their cells as a disciplinary action for not more than five days for administrative (115) violations and ten days for serious (115) violations.

Protective Housing Unit
If it is verified that an inmate's safety is in danger, he or she may request to be placed in a protective unit, or protective custody yard, where high-risk inmates are housed.

Involuntary Transfer
Inmate may be transferred if he or she routinely disrupts safety or if he or she is an identified gang member.

Source: California Department of Corrections and Rehabilitation. 2003.

ated a taxonomy of inmate violence (see Table 6.2). The term "mutual combat" is a CDCR term used to describe a fight between two men who assault each other. Interviewees also use this term. If one man hits or assaults another and the victim does not fight back, the CDCR calls it an "assault," and the victim is not written up. Interviewees described a riot as a large-scale fight between many (usually four or more) men in a public area.

Riots escalate and, as discussed in Chapter 3, quickly divide men by race. The men I interviewed explained that they avoided riots for two reasons. First, they are dangerous. Men use rocks or homemade weapons (e.g., shanks), and serious injuries are common. Second, after a riot, the prison is locked down and men are confined to their quarters until the administration lets them out. Although the men described the CDCR 115 written sanction as "no big deal," the lockdown was a serious threat. A lockdown may last months or years and, even more important, interferes with illegal businesses.

If one gang member is locked up in solitary confinement, that has little effect on the gang's activities. However, if the whole prison is

---

Table 6.2 Taxonomy of Inmate Violence, Men's Prisons

What kind of violent behavior were you personally involved in?

Cell fights
Minor fights, usually over disrespect. Typically, this is a one-on-one fight that is quick and includes punching someone out. It takes place in the cell to avoid administrative interference and control and prevents a lockdown.

Taking someone out
Serious attack against someone that takes place in the yard or a blind spot where there are no windows and few guards

Mutual combat
An assault between two inmates that results in administrative interference and reprimand

Riots
Large-scale fights between numerous (or hundreds of) inmates. Riots can start, stop, and start in another area of the prison and result in many injuries and casualties as well as a lockdown and reprimands.

locked down, there is little communication among inmates. Inmates create many rules in order to avoid formal sanctions or lockdowns. Thus, inmate society is highly structured from several directions. Its members live in a total institution, where authority comes down from the top, yet they also remain loyal to friends and gang members. Therefore, inmates must learn all of the rules very quickly in order to avoid trouble.

Many people believe that prisons are war zones where riots are common. Just entering the prison yard means you are at risk of being seriously hurt. However, riots are uncommon, and the chance of being killed in prison is pretty slim. In fact, California has one of the largest prison systems in the United States, and on average, thirteen men die each year because of an assault or escape (California Department of Corrections and Rehabilitation 2007). Since 1980, a total of four employees (three correctional officers and one factory supervisor) have been killed by inmates in California state prisons (California Department of Corrections and Rehabilitation 2008b). To some degree, formal mechanisms of social control work.

A large body of research focuses on the concept of social control (Bursik and Grasmick 1993; Hagen, Merkens, and Boehnke 1995; Hirschi 1969; Kornhauser 1978; Sampson and Laub 1994; Taylor 1996, 1997). Drawing from this research, I define "formal mechanisms of social control" to mean any legal, legitimate action grounded in codified laws and mandates. Informal mechanisms develop through family and community structures and agreements. They generally control deviant behavior more effectively than laws.

Of course, violence can result from an absence of social controls. Travis Hirschi (1969) was the first to propose a comprehensive theory of social control that focuses on bonds and attachments rather than personal motivations for deviance. In the simplest of terms, people who have bonds with family and nondeviant friends are less likely to commit deviant acts, including violence. Hirschi theorized that attachment to nondeviant peers allowed us to internalize social norms. If we formed healthy attachments, then we became invested (Hirschi called this "commitment") in nondeviant behavior to maintain social order. Charles Tittle (1995) also suggested that we examine external controls to explain violence and deviance. However, he argued against Hirschi's theory by focusing on two central issues about control and deviance. First, people engage in deviant behavior as a way to escape or avoid mechanisms of control. Second, those who control others engage in deviant acts to extend their power. Therefore, a curvilinear relationship (U-shaped) forms between control and deviance, which Tittle calls "control balance." Simply put, if you graph power (X axis) and deviance (Y axis), those with all or no power are more likely to commit crime or violence.

The extensive work by Burt Useem and others (Goldstone and Useem 1999; Useem 1985; Useem, Camp, and Camp 1996; Useem and Kimball 1987, 1991; Useem and Piehl 2006) focused on institutional responses to inmate violence, particularly riots. Useem and Piehl (2006) found prisons to be highly controlled environments. The mass incarceration trend that began in the 1980s did not result in chaos behind bars. Instead, careful planning on the part of the administrative staff helped reduce riots and inmate fatalities.

In short, riots are rare, inmate fatalities are down, and correctional officers are less likely to be killed now than in previous years. There is little evidence that the mass incarceration trend produced ungovernable institutions. However, is social control at the ground level (informal mechanisms of control) possible in this total institution? Tittle (1995) argued that those with little power engage in deviant acts to empower themselves and control others. In the stories told throughout this book, interviewees stated that strength and power are advantageous for inmates. Among men, those showing weakness were victimized and remained at the bottom of the prison hierarchy. Among women, those who showed strength or outsmarted other inmates avoided many problems. Inmates have no institutional power, yet they go to great lengths to control each other. To explore this issue further, I examine the accounts, rationales, and stories of former inmates to understand their methods of control.

Cleaning Up Your Own Backyard

In Chapter 1, I noted that some inmates are automatically targeted for violence. Men who are child molesters or snitches are labeled "dirty" inmates. These men fall to the bottom of the prison hierarchy, which makes them deserving of violence in the eyes of the other inmates. Of course, these men can be taken to the protective custody (PC) yard, where they do not mingle with the other inmates. However, that creates its own problem: if men go to the PC yard, they cannot return to the general population because of the stigma associated with protective custody. Inmates will always label anyone coming from the PC yard as dirty. I asked men if anyone else is dirty, and some of them told me that they also target men who were convicted of a drive-by shooting. They described these men as cowards who were not manly enough to face the people they shot. Also, they endangered innocent victims and brought unwanted attention from the police.

A valid question is, how do inmates know about the crimes committed by their fellow inmates? Every person entering a California prison is given his or her court paperwork; inmates call this their "jacket." By law, they receive this paperwork so that they can use the law library to aid in their own appeal. As a man enters prison, another man (of the same race) approaches him and demands to see his jacket. For example, white men check the jackets of other white men in order to see why they were convicted. Interviewees explained that they knew the penal codes for "dirty" crimes such as child molestation. Of course, if a man refused to let others see his paperwork, the inmates assumed he was hiding something and he was labeled as dirty (Trammell and Chenault 2009). When male inmates decided someone was dirty, they informed their gang and set up a plan to assault or kill the dirty inmate. Interviewees also claimed that correctional officers told them about dirty inmates as well. This ritual ensured that there are few secrets in prison. Jose explained how this is done:

> JOSE: Everyone comes in with a jacket, it's like your paperwork that tells what you did, and so you have to show it to everyone, and if you don't then we all know what's up.
>
> TRAMMELL: What's up if you don't?
>
> JOSE: Then you did something you don't want to get around. Now, if you molest a kid, then you can lie and say you did something else, but then people find out.
>
> TRAMMELL : How?
>
> JOSE: The COs spill it or someone knows them or something. I've known guys that come in and keep to themselves, don't make any friends, and then someone will recognize them from another prison. They snitched on a gang member or something. It's obvious when someone's trying to hide something, you know?

According to Jose, inmates carefully watched each other in order to determine whom they can trust. In fact, this ritual forced men to trust one another enough to let others know why they were convicted. The fact that this is done by race makes this interaction especially interesting. If inmates decided someone was dirty, a member of his own race assaulted him. The men in my study stated that they did this to "clean up their own backyard." Roberto told me why: "It's about pride. You have to show pride and respect for your race. If a man hurts a child, a Mexican man, then he disrespects my race, and I need to step up. You know, if it is a Mexican man, he probably hurt a Mexican child, maybe his own child; I don't know. But I can't let the white men take care of that. I have to show that I care about my own." Anthony went even further: "Yes, I took one of those guys out. He raped a kid. A kid! He was a piece of white trash, let me tell you. The boys have a code: you take out your own. This proves that we're all on the same page with this shit. The boys come together over this and we all know who's dirty."

Assaulting dirty inmates symbolized pride about your race but also united the inmates. Men had to perform this act in order to show others that they took this rule seriously. In other words, to maintain a worthy identity, violence was necessary. In many ways, this form of violence was public because everyone knew if these men were assaulted. Interviewees explained that, many times, they had to remind gang members to take care of a dirty inmate. Roberto gave an example: "Sometimes we'd tell the blacks or the white guys to get on the ball and take care of their shit. We'd have to tell them, 'Hey, the COs said that guy is dirty; when are you taking care of business?'" Max told me this story:

> MAX: We had a dirty guy once. We got him in a blind spot, and three of us jumped him. Beat him down pretty bad.
>
> TRAMMELL: What was his race?
>
> MAX: White guy. We took care of the situation; there weren't many white guys in prison. There were a few that raped kids, but we got him. In fact, the blacks were always slow at taking care of a dirty guy. Some black guy comes on the yard. He's dirty, and the blacks let it slide. Don't they care about family and children? We'd have to get on their case about it. The Mexicans, they know the score, they're all about family and community.

Both Max and Geraldo criticized blacks for not taking care of "dirty" inmates quickly enough, though Geraldo was more tolerant:

> There are a lot of blacks in prison and some are good, God-fearing guys. They know to take care of their own. They get with the program. The religious ones are good guys, good Christian men. But overall, they don't stick with each other, not like we do. They don't care about taking care of their own race, taking out their own. The Mexicans will always fight for the brown people, but the blacks won't, they won't stick together.

A common theme emerged from these stories. These men clearly believed that they must take out dirty inmates to protect children and their community. However, this ritual transformed into a way to keep other gangs in check. They all agreed that child molesters were worthy of violence. They created a ritual to determine why men were convicted, and then they made sure that certain inmates were punished. If gangs were slow or reluctant to do so, men labeled it a weakness of their race. In other words, there was a racial hierarchy, and those who did not perform violence "for their race" were publicly ridiculed for not doing so. In this case, violence only helped your public image. Bobby described the planning: "The leaders told us, you have to take that guy to a blind spot; you have to take him out. We have no choice here. The clock is ticking, and everyone knows what has to be done. I do what my leader says, and if you do it quickly, you get credit for that on the yard. The boys know when a dirty guy is hit, and you're like a hero."

Although some of the men told me that African Americans were reluctant to take out the child molesters, African American men I interviewed, such as Daryl, discussed the importance of cleaning up their own backyard: "If it's a black guy, then we have to take care of him. I want to do it, or I want another black dude to do it. The white guys have no business hurting the black guys in prison." Angelo noted how quickly word got around in these situations: "We jumped this dude once. He killed his own kid, and he was dirty. He was on the yard maybe two days and we got him. I think it was a record or something. Even the skinheads were impressed. We never saw the dude again; he was out of the picture." By having a common cause, these men mobilized to informally punish dirty inmates. In addition, this ritual was a test for inmates, who had to prove that they were capable of serious acts of violence in order to show pride in their race. If, for any reason, you refused, you were siding with, if not protecting, child molesters. Of course, that kind of alliance was totally unacceptable and seriously damaged an inmates' identity.

The norm of segregation made race a salient characteristic, which facilitated blaming a specific group because some men refused to attack child molesters. For many men in prison, cleaning up their own backyard solidified their loyalty to their gang and their race. That, in turn, allowed these men to maintain a worthy identity. Approximately 1,300 men entered these prisons after being convicted of "lewd acts with a minor" (Trammell and Chenault 2009). Inmates are not actually killing all these men. However, they distance themselves from these offenders and manage their own public identity by showing that they are committed to punishment for dirty inmates.

Cleaning up their own backyard also meant handling problems with fellow gang members. Of course, gang members protected each other.

However, if one man brought unwanted attention or causes problems, his fellow gang members would step in and control the situation. In other words, they forced men to behave and follow the rules. It could mean that they allowed other gang members to beat him up without retaliating. Ramon explained how he had to turn over a fellow gang member who ran up a drug debt:

> We need to keep the boys in line. If one of our guys is a hothead or something and is always shooting off his mouth, it can get everyone into trouble. We don't want a lockdown. We don't want a riot. So I've had to beat down my own guys to control the bigger picture. If one of my guys is messing up, then we either offer him up to the other guys, or we take him down ourselves. Like I had a guy that ran up a big drug debt; he owed money to the woods [Peckerwood skinhead gang], and I had to turn him over to them. They took him to a cell and really beat the shit out of him. We had to do it. If not, then everyone fights.

Under other circumstances, gang members will defend each other and retaliate against anyone who hurts one of their own. Yet these men put their gangs in jeopardy with other gangs or the prison staff. Daniel gave an example of how checking gang members reduced problems between white and Mexican gangs:

> Yeah, we had a guy who, I don't know what his problem was. He always said shit in the yard to the Mexicans. I think he always thought that we would have his back. We'll take care of you, but there are limits, you know? You stick up for your own, but you don't start shit for no reason. He got jumped in a blind spot by the Mexican guys, and we were like, "Dude, that's what you get," you get no sympathy from us.

Bobby told me that it is advantageous for the men to keep the peace: "If you start shit and put us at risk, we'll turn you over. Do not fuck up our operation, you know? We ran some stuff in prison, and I am not going to let some retard piss off the colored guys cuz he can't control himself. We have to control our own shit." They clean up their own backyard in order to avoid dealing with the staff or causing fights. Angelo started some fights with members of a Mexican gang. His shot-caller asked him to stop making trouble. When he continued picking fights, his own gang members beat him up:

> ANGELO: The problem is that the incident—it's not even a real fight—
> is now going to turn the blacks against the Mexicans. There's going

> to be big trouble, a riot or something, so they can't have that. So two days later, the blacks come after me. Three guys sucker-punched me and knocked me down and beat me down.
>
> TRAMMELL: Were you hurt?
>
> ANGELO: Broke three fingers and my nose. I thought I might lose an eye cuz I couldn't see anything when it started, but it was just blood and stuff in my eyes. They had to do it; it was for the greater good, so to speak.
>
> TRAMMELL: Why?
>
> ANGELO: If they didn't do it, then there's trouble between the blacks and the Mexicans. I can't have that over my head. I mean [laughs], am I glad I got my ass beat? No. But it probably saved lives or at the very least, stopped a lockdown. They had to show the Mexicans that the problem is solved and that I learned a lesson.

There are three reasons why men informally punished each other. First, leaders wanted to control the behaviors of fellow gang members. They created a vertical hierarchy and used military terms (soldiers, lieutenants, etc.) to organize their gangs. To a large degree, the men must respect this pecking order. For the sake of harmony, they did not want conflict within the gang. Second, they needed to keep the peace between the gangs. One gang sells drugs and makes other deals with other gangs, and these transactions must go smoothly. Third, fights brought unwanted attention to the gangs. If they fought, they could go into a lockdown or have their cells searched. In other words, it was imperative that men enforce informal norms in order to avoid formal reprimands.

If cells were locked down, they could not sell their illegal drugs. If their cells were searched, they might lose their contraband or other illegal items. At the end of the day, it was in their best interest to maintain peace and reduce the visibility of violence. It was important that everyone follows the rules.

Private Spaces

If violence is necessary, men must find a way to reduce their chances of getting caught. Of course, they sometimes did get caught. Jose told me what happens:

> JOSE: If you get a serious 115 you get a CTQ [confinement to quarters] or go to the hole. Yeah, also you can lose your good time. Usually you go into the hole for a few weeks or so; it depends. It's not a big

deal, really. I got six 115s the last time I was in, and most of the time, it's over stupid stuff.

TRAMMELL: So you didn't care about being written up?

JOSE: Not really; it's not like they can do too much to you. I never thought about it too much. I really didn't like going to the hole, but whatever, it was only for a little while. I'm sure my file had some really interesting stuff in it. You should read it.

Juan told me about an unplanned fight:

JUAN: I got into a fight once and the cops broke it up, and we both got written up and two weeks in the hole. I didn't start the fight, but it did get out of hand and we—it wasn't planned—so we were in an open area. It was dumb, but we took care of business and I only got a 115, so no worries.

TRAMMELL: No worries? It's not a big deal?

JUAN: Oh, no, what else can they do to me? I'm already locked up, serving my time, dealing with the politics of prison, so the cops, well, they can't do much else to me. I don't worry about going to the hole or anything.

Almost all of these men (95 percent) stated that they fought in prison, and the chance of being written up did not deter them from acting out. Daniel explained that, with his long sentence, he had no incentive to avoid fighting:

I must have gotten into twenty fights in prison, and I got a few write-ups for them. They finally transferred me out because of fighting, which was fine by me. I got a ten-year sentence; you think I'm not going to get into a few scuffles? Come on, man, give me a break. They can't do much to you, it's not like I serve two years and parole right? I know I'm serving like 85 percent of my time, so to hell with it, I'm not playing nice or anything.

Of course, they also hated solitary confinement. This form of punishment is particularly brutal because they never knew what day it was, and they spoke to no one. Clearly, they enjoyed socializing with other inmates, and, as Jake explained, going to the hole was a painful process. "You know, they threw me in the hole once for three weeks. That was pretty bad. It's just about the worst thing I've ever dealt with, but I survived it, and my boys were waiting for me when I got out. I guess they have to separate us for fighting; I get that, no hard feelings [laughs]." Brad seconded his opinion: "There's nothing worse than going to the hole. You go crazy after a while. I swear that I saw things and heard things that I knew weren't there. I was in for like, six days, and I really thought I'd go nuts."

Clearly, there are several problems with public fighting. Inmates risk going to solitary confinement and/or a lockdown. Also, they could get written up. At the same time, they got into trouble with their fellow gang members if they randomly assaulted another inmate, because it could bring unwanted attention to their gang. Therefore, men solved this problem by privatizing violence. They told me that, in order to keep things quiet, they had a "cell fight" in which two or three inmates punch each other in a cell. The cell is a popular place to fight because they rarely get caught and getting some aggression out prevents dangerous riots. If they punch someone in the yard, it escalates. If they "take it to the cell," the fight is quick and quiet. Adam told me this story:

> TRAMMELL: How many cell fights did you get in?
>
> ADAM: Oh, man, tons . . . probably ten or so.
>
> TRAMMELL: Tell me about one you had.
>
> ADAM: I got into it with my cellie. He took my stuff and then denied it; who else would have it, right? So I saw him in the yard, and I told him that we need to meet up in the cell and take care of business. We go there, and I beat him down.
>
> TRAMMELL: Was he hurt?
>
> ADAM: Nah, we just knocked each other around a bit. I hit him; he hit me, nothing serious.

Samuel said that he once used a cell fight to relieve some tension:

> Prison is rough. We live under a lot of pressure to be tough, and it's, well, it's tough. Things build up, and we need a way to take care of the little things before they become big things. One time, I had a guy that called me a nigger. I've heard that a hundred times in my life, but it hit me on the wrong day. I'd really had a tough day, so I followed him to his cell and beat his ass. I couldn't do anything in the yard; we had to take it to the cell, but let me tell you, I felt so much better after it was over. It was like, "Damn, that felt good." I slept great that night.

Anthony explained that "usually, you settle the dumb stuff there. If someone disses me or someone takes my stuff, then the leaders tell us to take it to the cell. We slug it out and get things taken care of. I probably had seven or eight fights in prison."

Obviously, inmates tried to avoid formal reprimands and solitary confinement. These men used their cell fights to create a private space for violent action. Of course, this meant that they must keep quiet about their fight and not seek medical help. Martino told me this story about one of his cell fights:

> TRAMMELL: What happened?
>
> Martino: I think I may have broke his jaw. I punched him first, and he and I really went at it. He lost a tooth and couldn't talk for a while, so I think I broke his jaw.
>
> TRAMMELL: Did you see a doctor?
>
> Martino: No, if we did, then we're busted for fighting. So we punched each other until we got tired and then we just sat and stared at each other until we fell asleep. It was a good thing. We got things out, and we didn't get in trouble. The problem is that there's no way to get this stuff out without getting written up.

Although they had very little privacy in prison, they found blind spots and used their cells to control the level of violence. Of course, they sometimes did fight in the yard. Interviewees explained that shot-callers would decide if, and when, a public fight was necessary. However, the men who spoke with me seemed genuinely invested in maintaining a peaceful environment. Although they claimed to not care about getting a 115 violation, they avoided formal reprimands when they could.

Nonviolent Solutions

As I showed earlier in this book, men claimed that fights often started over theft, race, drugs, and disrespect. If one man disrespected another, there was a chance that he would have to apologize to him in a public place like the yard. These men stated that such apologies resolved many issues. Seth described what happened:

> Sometimes you fight just because someone pissed you off. If someone pisses me off, you know, starts trouble with me; he has to answer to his own people. They decide if it's worth fighting over, you know? If they decide that he's just a big dick and he needs to apologize to me

for being a dick, then he will tell me he's sorry. That's how it usually ends. Nothing too dramatic.

According to Adam, the shot-caller sometimes talked with fellow gang members about his decision:

> ADAM: The shot-caller picks the people that do vote. They make a group conscience and they vote and they get the key holder, and he gives you the green light or the red light.
>
> TRAMMELL: They decide if you fight?
>
> ADAM: Yeah, let's say I'm wrong and I disrespected someone, then they tell me to apologize, but if I'm right and I was disrespected, then he would say let's get the rat pack and we go in for the fight.

Samuel explained how smart leaders take care of these problems:

> If the leaders are smart, they talk with their guys. A good leader is someone who has been in prison a while and knows what's up. He will make sure all of his boys are on board with any stuff that goes down. He will settle the small stuff quietly and let the dogs loose to fight when you gotta fight. The important thing is that he knows the difference; he knows when to back off and when to attack.

These stories intrigued me for several reasons. First, they showed that inmates knew that violence was not the answer to all their problems. There was a time and place for everything, and these men needed to learn when to fight and when to apologize. In other words, leaders evaluated the social context and decided the appropriate course of action.

Second, the men in my study told me that conflict was often resolved with an apology. In some cases, shot-callers worked together to decide who disrespected whom and make the offender apologize to the other man. For the most part, men abided by these decisions and shook hands and apologized in order to avoid trouble. These gangs are violent and responsible for the prison drug trade. However, it appears that they are also organizing everyone's social life, which means schooling the men to accept the informal norms of prison culture. If they breached these norms, they were punished, sometimes violently. However, men learned to remain loyal to their gang leaders and to follow instructions.

As these men worked and played together in prison, they developed strategies based on the expectations of the existing prison culture. Violence was a valid strategy until it became a liability. As the prison administration worked to stabilize prisons and reduce violence, these men developed strategies to reflect their rules. To some extent, their choice reduced violence because the men avoided riots in order to keep prison staff at bay. However, it also privatized violent behavior and caused inmates to devise and enforce rules about who fights with whom.

This performance is very important. Misbehaving inmates must apologize to one another publicly or take their fights to their cells. The audience is watching to see how gangs deal with conflict. In the context of a business transaction, peace is necessary. Using centralized leaders promotes social cohesion and provides protection. Of course, leaders demand cooperation and loyalty. That is one reason why leaders are sometimes willing to turn over their own men for violent punishment. They cannot lose control of the situation and allow men to do whatever they want.

Previous research has focused on formal methods of control (Useem, Camp, and Camp 1996; Useem and Piehl 2006). There is little doubt that prison administrators worked hard to control this environment. However, these men also worked hard to control their lives. As Tittle (1995) pointed out, those with little power are more likely to use violence to gain power. From the stories told by these men, it seems clear that inmates are willing to use violence, even against their own men, in order to gain power. They structure their gangs in a way that allows men to use violence "for the greater good" because too much violence brings unwanted attention from prison staff. In other words, they lose power if the prison staff tightens their grip.

Formal Sanctions in Women's Prisons

As pointed out in Chapter 5, women used rumors and gossip as a method of social control. Of course, women also faced formal sanctions for their bad behavior. A key difference between the men and women I interviewed is that women were more likely to complain about the number of written violations they received. They also stated that they received many administrative 115 violations and very few serious violations (see Table 6.1). The latter include misuse of food, destroying property, and so on. Judy told me about one of her violations: "I got a 115 once for cutting off my pants. They hadn't given us any shorts and it was hotter than hell, so I cut my pants to make shorts. I got an administrative 115 for it, no big deal." Alexandria remembered that she received approximately twenty administrative violations and only one serious violation: "Oh, boy, they write you up for everything. You get written up if your clothes are torn, if you're late to work. I get it; some of that is necessary. But I was once written up for breaking up a fight. Two women went at it, and I separated them. Why should I get in trouble for doing the right thing?"

Only two men in my study remembered getting an administrative violation while in prison. However, every woman in my study told me that they had received many violations (in some cases dozens of them) for hiding food, swearing, or tearing their clothes. Prison staff walked around the halls with pads and pens and wrote them up for every infraction. Sofia told me a story about how she was written up for destroying state property:

> I never got in any real trouble for fighting or hurting people. I got written up a bunch of times for stupid shit. I got a bad sunburn once cuz I didn't have any sunblock. I'm white as a ghost, right? Well, they put us in the yard, and I got a serious sunburn with blisters and stuff. I asked for medical care cuz I really felt sick from the burn. I couldn't work, so they gave me a 115 for being sunburned. They said that I destroyed state property by burning myself. I never got any medical treatment for it either.

Interviewees did not complain about getting into trouble. In fact, they stated that they did not get into real trouble but were reprimanded for minor offenses. In Sofia's case, she stated that, because staff could not find any legitimate cause for complaint when she could not work, they reprimanded her for "destroying state property," which implied that she was state property. That kind of behavior only served to remind these women that they were prisoners and to remind them that they were constantly being watched.

As Judy and Alexandria pointed out, they received so many of these violations that they became meaningless because they never amounted to anything. Mia told me this story:

> Oh boy, I got . . . fifty violations. Yeah, at least fifty. One time, I got written up for swearing. I said "shit." I didn't threaten anyone or anything; it wasn't like that. I was telling a joke and said "shit," and the guard wrote me up. I told her that I could not believe she was doing that, and she told me to act ladylike and this won't happen again. I tell you, I cursed up a storm when I got away from her.

Apparently, Mia was not hurting anyone, nor was she causing trouble. In fact, she was joking with some fellow inmates, so there was no threat to safety. More interesting is the response from the correctional officer to act "ladylike" in prison. That response has more to do with curbing "unladylike" behavior than with controlling the environment. Similarly, Alexandria complained that she was written up for trying to stop a fight. Of course, that was not her job, and she could have gotten hurt. However, in these cases, women were trying to get along with others or prevent problems, and still they were formally reprimanded. Barbara told me about one of her violations:

> This woman and I were talking about spanking kids. We both are mothers, and she believes in spanking and I don't. We talked about it for a while, and she said something like, "Don't you want to keep your kids out of prison? You have to spank them to discipline them." I told her that she is stupid; violence isn't necessary and stuff like that. I guess we got loud. We weren't yelling or anything, but we raised our voices, I guess. They came over and asked us what was going on. They heard me call her "stupid," and they wrote me up for disrespect.

From what the men told me, disrespect was a common cause of violence. However, they sometimes controlled the violence by having men apologize to the people they disrespected. According to Barbara, correctional officers overheard her conversation and wrote her up. Of course, that did nothing to make things right between Barbara and the woman she was talking to. She was not made to apologize, and there was no real intervention about their conflict. It is possible that this argument could have led to violence. At the same time, no one was addressing the actual problem.

These administrative write-ups seem to be one way that the prison administration deals with real, or imagined, problems. I do not mean to discount the need for formal reprimands, yet the women in my study could not effectively explain their function. Instead, they stated that it was a way for prison staff to interfere with their lives. Marilyn described what she saw as their true intent: "You know, they gave us so many of these pieces of paper, it was a joke. I think they do it because they have to show that they are controlling us. We rarely fight and don't ever riot, so they pick the piddly stuff to go crazy about. They just want to boss us around." Marilyn is not incorrect in pointing out that women commit less violence than men. In that sense, women are probably easier to control, so Marilyn's opinion is valid. Why would staff use administrative 115 forms in these cases? One explanation is that they interpreted her behavior as a real problem for women. Swearing and yelling may be so common in men's prison that staff rarely notice these behaviors. However, these women were expected to behave in accordance with traditional gender norms. Therefore, this behavior stands out to the prison staff.

Intimidation and Control

The men in this study claimed that they had no relationship with correctional officers and worked hard to avoid them. Some women told me that they were afraid of prison officials, whereas others believed that they were good men and women who were simply doing their jobs. No one in my study said that he or she was sexually abused by any of the prison staff. The women who were intimidated by the correctional officers, such as Ella, stated that their fear of these officers curbed their deviant behavior.

> They like to intimidate you. They like to throw their weight around. They like to act like the boss. They would get on a rampage and tear up my cell. They never touched me or anything. They never said anything threatening, but they let you know who's boss. I just ignored them. You don't talk with them anyway. I hear stories about how they abuse women, sexual stuff, but I figured if I stayed out of their way and did what they told me to do, I'd be fine, so that's what I did. They're big guys; you don't want to make them mad.

Molly felt that the staff regularly abused women:

> I know that some of the COs pat women down and feel them up and shit. It's gross. It's like, we have no control over our lives: we get with men that abuse us, pimp us out, get us on drugs. Then we get busted for something that we may or may not have done, probably because our husbands or boyfriends get us into this stuff, and then we get to jail and then a CO feels us up. My God, they are horrible men; they scared me to death. I jumped out of my skin every time one patted me down, which happens all the time.

Both Molly and Ella felt violated and helpless because they lost control over their own lives. Nether of these women claimed that prison staff abused them. It was the mere threat of abuse that controlled them. They were very careful to follow the rules in order to avoid correctional officers. Of course, men go to great lengths to avoid them as well. However, that does not curb their deviant behavior; instead, they try to circumvent formal rules.

Since the early 1990s, there have been cases in which correctional officers assaulted female inmates (Burton-Rose 2003; Human Rights Watch 2001; Human Rights Watch Women's Rights Project 1996; Smith 1998; Talvi 2003). According to a 2001 Human Rights Watch report:

Sexual abuse against women by correctional officers remained wide-spread despite new laws prohibiting it and greater public awareness of the problem. A federal circuit court upheld federal legislation, the Prison Litigation Reform Act, that bars lawsuits by inmates seeking damages for mental or emotional injury suffered while in custody where there is no proof of significant physical injury. This restriction on the ability of inmates to vindicate their rights in court was one of many ways in which US laws and judicial mechanisms failed to meet the standards mandated by the Convention against Torture. (Human Rights Watch 2001:11)

The majority of correctional officers in the United States are men (Britton 2003), and some women worry about having these men control their lives and their bodies. Furthermore, over half of the women in prison are victims of physical and sexual abuse (Chesney-Lind 2002), which heightens their awareness of and reaction to abuse. Therefore, Molly and Ella's fears were not irrational. Also, women are less likely to be violent, so there is no need to use a lot of force with them.

Alexandria criticized the attitude of correctional officers: "A lot of women get along with them, but they scared me. They act like we're all a bunch of ax murderers and so they do a lot of bullying. Women are no threat to them. We aren't going to attack them, why do they have to act like such jerks? Just treat us like people, you know." Karla explained how she felt dehumanized by her experiences in prison: "The COs come into your cell; they steal your stuff. They confiscate your clothes and make up some reason why they'll take your stuff. They threaten you and tell you they'll make your life miserable. It's no joke. I've been hit by them, you know, knocked around. They harass the young girls; you know they want them to give it up." Olivia told me that male correctional officers try to intimidate women:

They all have a power trip; almost all of them are on a trip. I've known a few that I could have a discussion with, but when it comes down, they are the CO and I'm the inmate. They aren't my friends, and that's the way it is. They all . . . instead of just having you do your time, they want to make it hard on you. They take this attitude that "It's my job to make it hard on you so you won't come back," and it's like, "No, that's not your job." They would say, "I'm the authority figure." Well, big deal, you don't scare me [laughs]. Some women are scared of these guys, but I think it's all a bluff, you know.

These women explain that intimidation is a method of social control. As with the stories about administrative reprimands, women were reminded that they had no control over their lives and were being watched.

They stated that the only way to avoid trouble is to stay out of trouble. In that sense, women are much easier to deal with than men.

At the same time, some women claimed not to be bothered by these men at all. Mia asserted that women often lie about sexual abuse:

> Most of the men in there, they are not into it. They don't want to have anything to do with us. They just want to do their time, go home and stuff. Why would they risk their job and stuff for a blowjob? They can get that outside. Women lie about this all the time. If any woman tells you that she was raped or harassed in prison, she lies. The men are good guys, mostly churchy types. Women wish these guys would rape them.

Sofia described a pat-down:

> If they suspect that someone has some contraband or something, they make everyone line up and pat them down. Now they are supposed to keep their hands flat and use the backs of their hands to check you for drugs or weapons or whatever, but these guys will just grope you, feel your breasts. Then you see women getting in line twice for this treatment. I mean, what the hell is that about? We can't really expect guys to respect us when women enjoy it and ask for more.

Stephanie would get angry with women who flirted with correctional officers. She felt especially sorry for their husbands waiting for them to be released on parole:

> We get mad at some of the girls who flirt with these guys and stuff. I used to tell women to shut up about the cops. Those guys aren't bothering them, so shut up about it. I know they miss their husbands or boyfriends and stuff. That's the thing. These women have men on the outside; these poor guys are waiting at home with them and some of these women really embarrass themselves with the COs. I think they just want attention.

As I pointed out in Chapter 4, women often blamed other women who breached prison norms. Some claimed that women lost their right to say no to sex because they entered into a mutually advantageous relationship. Sofia and Stephanie made similar claims about women who flirted with correctional officers. Sofia went so far as to state that this behavior hurt all women because correctional officers might lose respect for the inmates.

What seems clear from their statements is that formal and informal norms work well to control these women. Correctional officers made sure that female inmates knew they were being watched and were quick to reprimand them for things such as swearing, disrespect, and torn clothing. Women like Mia, Sofia and Stephanie were quick to blame women who had inappropriate relationships with men. Informal social controls, such as rumors and gossip, also worked quite well. They enforced norms about appropriate inmate behavior and punished women who breached these norms.

Conclusion

To some extent, social control mechanisms work if they target something that the inmate values. For example, the men seemed to be very concerned about avoiding a lockdown so they could run their illegal businesses, whereas the women valued their friendships and wanted to avoid trouble. A key difference between the men and women I talked to is that, for women, the fear of correctional staff curbed some of their behavior. Men, however, created a set of rituals used to skirt institutional control.

What is particularly interesting about my interview data is the way in which men defined and described deviance. They created social arrangements around the economic structures of underground businesses. They informally punished those who transgressed norms by using violence. Furthermore, they described these arrangements as positive and claimed to save lives. In other words, they redefined deviant behavior as anything that subverted their informal social arrangements, so much so that they assaulted those who worked directly with prison staff (snitches) and "offered up" fellow gang members to rival gangs to show that everyone was on board with this arrangement. Whether or not these rules actually reduced violence falls outside the scope of this book. However, there is no doubt that male inmates were organized, structured, and faithful to informal social controls.

There are several explanations for the fact that men and women received different types of violations. First, women commit fewer acts of violence. Therefore, they represent less of a threat than the men. Simply put, men will receive more serious violations because they commit more serious offenses. Second, the staff attenuates to problems they see on a regular basis. Those who supervise men are probably concerned about gangs, the drug trade, and racial violence. Although these things are present in women's prisons, they are serious problems only for men. If men swear or disrespect each other, staff might not notice or care. In other words, they cannot attenuate to all the problems, so they focus on the more serious issues. As others have pointed out, women are expected to adhere to gender norms and face sanctions if they fail to do so (Gillespie 2000; Girshick 2000; Stanko 2001). This is a key difference between men and women. Women are expected to act "ladylike," but men get away with things like swearing or being sunburnt. The bar for "decent" behavior is raised for women, who are being sanctioned for not acting in accordance with their prescribed gender norms.

In other words, the staff in women's prison might be concerned about the minor infractions because they are trying to curb behavior that they deem unfeminine. They might believe that "unladylike" behavior is the precursor to crime and violence. That being said, formal controls work differently for women than men. For men, formal control is seen as a challenge. For women, formal control is described as another layer of abuse and humiliation.

What does this tell us about prison culture? Tittle was correct (1995) to assume that those with little power will use violence to gain power. However, a person's use of violence depends on whether or not he or she is socialized to believe that violence is an option. Those who study gender state that prescribed gender norms dictate that women are less physically aggressive than men (Cahill 1989; Connell 1987, 2000; Thorne 1998). These women claimed that they were never "taught" to be aggressive or use violence, which limited their strategies in prison. Of course, some women used violence against fellow inmates. Interviewees were quick to point out that they were acting like men. This indicates that they believe violent action is a masculine trait.

When challenged with the burden of formal sanctions, men created rituals and used violence to circumvent these sanctions. Women, however, would usually behave. In both cases, their performances were validated by the response of their peers. Women's identity was threatened if they flirted with correctional officers or caused trouble. Men's identity was damaged if they brought unwanted attention to their gang activities. Therefore, both men and women must perform in accordance with informal rules in order to maintain a worthy identity.

7

Where Do We Go from Here?

In this book, I examined how men and women described and justified prison violence. Specifically, I focused on how violence was justified within the confines of inmate culture. In doing so, I paid particular attention to issues surrounding race, gender, and social control. This book contributes to the vast prison literature by examining violence and culture from the perspective of the inmate. Interviewees often described physical and sexual violence as part of the prison experience. They also described violence as a problem but downplayed their own behavior. I found it interesting that they described violence as a necessary tool of social control. In this sense, they believed that everyone needs to follow the rules.

My goal was to discuss these issues at a time when many Americans are taking a long, hard look at the prison system and asking important questions about the exact function of this institution. Currently, lawmakers in some states are deciding if they want to continue supporting mass incarceration or explore other, less expensive ways to address crime. At the same time, we are finally paying attention to the problem of sexual violence in prison and taking steps to reduce sexual abuse. All these things are headed in the right direction. We should make these institutions safe and productive instruments of change. But in order to do so, we need to understand what goes on in these facilities from the perspective of the inmates. If we want to promote a "culture of mutual respect," as outlined by the Commission on Safety and Abuse in America's Prisons (Gibbons and Katzenbach 2006), we should understand what the inmates value and respect. We should try to see things from their perspective. If we want to change their attitudes and behaviors, we need to understand their attitudes and behaviors.

Prison Culture

Culture is based on norms, rules, artifacts, and language created and used by people within any given society. Prison is really a subculture where men and women create their own norms and rules. Throughout this book, I presented the stories of men and women who learned to survive in prison. They mentored each other and socialized new inmates to teach them valuable survival skills. These skills became engrained into prison culture as people learned valuable coping mechanisms and informal rules. To be sure, cultural norms change as new inmates enter prison, especially in the recent mass incarceration era. Culture is not a standardized set of rules that are universal and unbending. Rather, inmates learn to adapt and thrive in an environment that is supposedly meant to rehabilitate them. This is an important point: we put people in prison to make them better people. We believe that, if punishment is harsh, inmates will be deterred from ever committing crime again. In reality, it seems as if inmates learn to sidestep formal rules and rely on informal methods of control to maintain order in prison.

Since the 1970s, Americans have declared a "war on drugs" and a "war on crime" that put millions of people behind bars (Parenti 1999; Reiman 2001; Sterling 1998; Tonry 1995; Wacquant 2001). Moreover, legislators lengthened prison sentences, which kept people in prison for long periods of time (Mauer and Chesney-Lind 2002; Tonry and Frase 2001). For example, "truth in sentencing laws" mandated that inmates serve up to 85 percent of their sentences rather than face parole boards earlier in their sentence. As Tonry (1999) points out in a report for the Department of Justice, this causes problems for prison officials who have limited resources. If inmates serve long sentences, it becomes expensive to rehabilitate them. In California, these resources were stretched so thin that a panel of federal judges ordered California prison administrators to release upward of 46,000 inmates (*Coleman v. Schwarzenegger* 2009; *Schwarzenegger v. Plata* 2010).

Of course, mass incarceration also affected prison culture. Men and women learned to adapt to their crowded environment by creating rules and rituals that, many times, forced inmates to get along with one another. Those rules did not eliminate violence. Inmates did, however, learn to avoid the problems associated with violence, such as formal reprimands and invasions of privacy. To be sure, their informal rules are probably a direct result of mass incarceration. This is but one collateral consequence of the tough-on-crime movement in the United States. We now have men and women behind bars who create rules that put a wall between themselves and prison staff, the people who are tasked with helping them rehabilitate. Of course, drawing on the stories told by interviewees, staff members who demean or bully inmates succeed only in driving them further away. We cannot blame the inmates alone for these problems.

The Issue of Control

In the previous chapters, I outlined several important issues worth noting. It seemed that the men and women I interviewed went to great lengths to avoid violence in prison. Men explained how they avoided riots, and women claimed to have carefully followed instructions given to them by correctional officers. They do not describe prisons as chaotic or out of control. For these people, prison was their home. They made friends, had jobs, and in some cases, earned money from illegal businesses or prison jobs. This is probably surprising for many people reading this book. Many assume that we fill prisons with bad people, and therefore, they behave badly. Instead, inmates are invested in maintaining a safe prison environment.

One reason that inmates wanted peace is that they feared they would lose something. For example, men did not want to lose profits from their drug businesses because of a lockdown. Therefore, they controlled themselves and others in order to maintain their freedom. There are several interesting points that should be made about this issue. First, these inmates carefully made decisions based on the possible outcomes. They were not irrational people who were prone to violence just for the sake of violence. Instead, they cared about their environment and wanted some control over their own lives. This is especially important for people who have lost their freedom. In order to promote their semblance of control, they denounce the effectiveness of formal control and the authority of the prison staff.

Second, the system inmates set up highlights the fact that they can respond to rewards in a positive way. If they truly believe that they will lose something tangible, they are more likely to behave. Of course, not every inmate will behave under these circumstances. Also, there are some inmates who will always prey on others for their own sadistic gratification. However, inmates coordinated their efforts and maintained order if they truly believed that they would benefit from these actions.

Also, the fact that every man in my study described correctional officers as useless speaks volumes. These men told themselves that they never truly lost control over their lives. In reality, they were under state supervision the entire time they were incarcerated. However, they believed that they ran the prisons and controlled each other. Furthermore, they believed that prison staff relied on their ability to control one another. Is it possible that, on some level, prison staff rely on the inmates, especially gang leaders, to help control each other? I think that is possible, but then it means that inmates are doing the job of prison staff. I think it is more likely that both inmates and prison staff enjoy the benefits of a structured environment. Therefore, there is a coordinated effort to maintain the peace. As much as former inmates denounce the legitimate power of the state, chaos is not an attractive alternative.

Some of the women liked the correctional officers and thought they tried to help the inmates. Others feared the correctional officers and avoided them at all cost. According to research since the 1990s, there are gender differences in how men and women experience fear (Hollander 2001), and men typically fear violence less than women (Goodey 1995; Valentine 1992). It is not too surprising that some of these women were scared of men who have complete control over their lives and their bodies. It seems logical that male correctional officers intimidate some female prisoners. Therefore, women behaved because they feared losing even more control over their own lives.

In order for inmates to maintain their cultural norms, they had to quickly socialize new inmates entering prison. They mentored each other, told each other the rules, sometimes gave each other "handbooks" about proper behavior, and then punished those who broke the rules. These are not the behaviors of people who want a society of chaos and violence. These are the behaviors of people who have lost all control over their lives and want to regain some of that control. On the negative side, the highly organized society set up by inmates strengthens the barrier between them and the institution and surely impedes the rehabilitation process.

Another intriguing finding is that interviewees described violence as a necessary evil. Violence was often used instrumentally, as a method of social control. More specifically, inmates used violence to avoid intrusion into their illegal businesses and to control problem inmates. In fact, men often became violent to punish those who brought unwanted attention into their lives. If inmates disrupted the social order, they put others at risk. Therefore, men must teach each other a lesson, sometimes using violence to do so. For some of the women, some gained power by adopting masculine traits. That way, they could control others by using force. The confines of gender socialization and gender norms affect prison culture, not always in a humane way.

Developing a Culture of Mutual Respect

According to the findings presented by the Commission on Safety and Abuse in America's Prisons (Gibbons and Katzenbach 2006:68):

> Another approach to institutional change targets the values, decisions, and behavior of the leaders and staff of the institution. In particular, there is increasing interest in the role that corrections officers play in setting the tone of an institution and, thereby, contributing to the behavior of prisoners. This approach focuses on staff training, problem solving, and the development of leaders who embrace and can model positive values and behaviors.

The Commission on Safety and Abuse in America's Prisons argues that prisons, as hierarchical institutions, dictate control and institutional values from the top down. Therefore, correctional officers, as representatives of this institution, must be humane and just in their actions. If they are, it will help promote a culture of mutual respect in prison. I agree with this argument. However, I also contend that, by focusing on the stories inmates tell us, we can identify what they value, which should also help coordinate a culture of mutual respect in prisons. Therefore, one way to improve the conditions of prison is to support research that focuses on mutual respect and conflict management.

We know little about how inmates and staff resolve conflict in a productive manner. It is important to note that prison administrators are sometimes unwilling to allow researchers into their facilities to collect data, for two main reasons. First, if researchers enter prisons, staff must work to assist and protect these researchers, which takes time away from their daily routines. Right now, resources are stretched thin. However, staff can gain a lot from this research. They might be able to ask for more state funds based on the recommendations of the research team. They may be able to focus attention on issues they were previously unaware of. Finally, they can evaluate their existing programs and make informed cuts or improvements to these programs. In the long run, research may save money and protect staff and improve efficiency. I would assume that every prison warden would appreciate good, solid research that makes his or her job easier.

A second reason why prison administrators might be unwilling to work with researchers is that they know they have problems and do not want to shine a light on these problems. Although I understand how they feel, that is not a valid reason to avoid researchers. If they have problems, they might benefit from fixing these problems. This could reduce the number of lawsuits and help rehabilitate the inmates. If correctional officers are instigating problems, they need to be dealt with or fired. If they have programs that do not work, they can improve or cut them.

Recently, lawmakers began admitting that they had made mistakes with regard to crime control in the United States. In May 2009, the head of the White House Office of Drug Control Policy, Gil Kerlikowske, called for an end to the "war" analogy for our drug policies: "Regardless of how you try to explain to people it's a 'war on drugs' or a 'war on a product,' people see a war as a war on them. . . . We're not at war with people in this country" (Fields 2009:A3). In September 2010, California governor Arnold Schwarzenegger signed Senate Bill 1449, which reduced the sentence for those caught with one ounce of marijuana or less from a misdemeanor to an infraction. In a letter to the California Senate, the governor stated: "This bill changes the crime of possession of less than an ounce of marijuana from a misdemeanor punishable only by a $100 fine to an infraction punishable by a $100 fine. Under existing law, jail time cannot be imposed, probation cannot be ordered, nor can the base fine exceed $100 for someone convicted of this crime" (Schwarzenegger 2010).

Of course, many drug laws are currently under scrutiny as states struggle to find money to arrest and incarcerate people for drug possession. What is especially interesting is that, for the first time since we declared war on drugs, elected officials are willing to admit that we made mistakes. Public leaders no longer describe mass incarceration as "success" but rather as a problem that needs fixing. For example, in 2007 the Texas legislature expanded drug courts and drug programs and revised parole practices to help reduce the inmate population in the state. John Whitmire, state senator from Houston, explained: "Our violent offenders, we lock them up for a very long time—rapists, murderers, child molesters. The problem was that we weren't smart about nonviolent offenders. The legislature finally caught up with the public" (Liptak 2008:B2). Clearly, prison administrators can learn from their mistakes and fix problems in their system. There is nothing to be gained by shutting out researchers who are willing to collect data in prison.

We could give inmates incentives for working hard through the system. If inmates complete programs in prison, such as GED or drug and alcohol counseling, this may prepare them for parole. If we identify and reinforce their positive traits (working hard, making money), we could give them incentives to avoid violence and maintain control. In other words, if we offer inmates (both men and women) viable options to make money, they should respond in a positive manner. This means offering real job training and working with community members to accept parolees into their businesses.

To build social skills and reduce conflict, we could create prison programs that build relationships grounded in mutual trust and cooperation. Sociological studies have shown that in-group dynamics are very strong and you can promote pro-social behavior and cooperation through team-building activities (Tajfel and Turner 1979; Vaghan, Tajfel, and Williams 1981). As humans, we seem to naturally divide into groups and quickly see the out-group, or the other, as different and bad. If we can create programs that encourage cooperation and rewards, it may facilitate change.

In many states, volunteer groups work with inmates. For example, in California, the Kairos Prison Ministry Program created prison programs to help inmates develop healthy relationships in prison. Perhaps it is time to evaluate these programs to determine their effectiveness. If these programs are working to build community, why not institutionalize them to include a wider variety of inmates? We could create secular programs that could help non-religious inmates. I realize that many people would want to discourage community building in prison. However, these inmates have already created their own society and subculture. Why would we not help them create more functional and productive social networks?

Of course, some prison administrators have worked hard to build a positive prison community. For example, in April 2000, the Department of Justice, Office of Justice Programs hosted a Learned Hate Round Table meeting to explore hate crimes in US prisons. Those attending made several interesting discoveries. They discussed the fact that every prison system holds people who are hostile toward the "other." There are no bias-free prisons. Also, in some prisons, the staff takes an active role in reducing hostility between the inmates (Meachum 2000:132):

> Sheryl Ramstad Hvass, commissioner of the Minnesota Department of Corrections, instructed correctional officers to assign seating for inmates in the cafeteria to prevent inmates from self-segregating and rejecting unwelcome table partners. She reported that, at first, the officers were annoyed at having to serve as "maître d's" of the cafeteria, but have realized the positive effect this practice has had on dis-

ruptions and tensions that had occurred during mealtimes. Now, staff
and inmates alike praise this intervention.

This is one small step that worked to reduce problems during mealtime.
Of course, the men in my study claimed that they would not integrate
under any circumstance. Therefore, in a system like California's, prison
staff would need to work on the larger problem of long-standing segregation and racial hostility.

In the aftermath of an eleven-day race riot that resulted in the murder of a correctional officer, the Ohio Department of Rehabilitation and
Correction (DRC) made a concerted effort to reduce racism and hostility in its prison system. Inmates claimed that the riot was caused by
forced racial integration (Wilkinson and Unwin 1999). In response, the
Ohio DRC hired more minority correctional officers. Employees were
trained to handle and defuse hostile situations surrounding race, ethnicity, and religion. When the staff are more tolerant and show respect to
all people, they are modeling appropriate behavior for the inmates
(Wilkinson and Unwin 1999). Another important change included the
creation of cultural diversity programs for the inmates. These programs
cover a wide variety of issues. For example, they devoted the months of
February and March to multicultural activities. This way, they do not
focus on one ethnic celebration (i.e., Cinco de Mayo). Instead, they created inclusive programs to help bring all people together. Of course,
prison staff must be dedicated to promoting diversity and cultural understanding for these kinds of programs to work:

> One of the most compelling examples of the success of diversity for
> inmates is seeing the presence of a diverse staff, particularly manage-
> ment staff. Correctional managers must practice what they preach by
> recruiting and retaining qualified staff that represent a wide variety of
> cultures and experiences. Again, while taking black and white into ac-
> count is important, so are the contributions of females, older staff, em-
> ployees from various ethnic backgrounds and those espousing
> different religions and beliefs. (Wilkinson and Unwin 1999:100)

It is very difficult, if not impossible, to completely eliminate racial
and ethnic bias, but prison administrators can take steps to reduce problems and help make their facilities more functional. It is not something
that can be done with one program; it will take an ongoing, coordinated
effort involving dedicated people who are committed to change. In fact,
the California Department of Corrections and Rehabilitation should
make it clear that all staff must be dedicated to institutional change.
They should not be waiting until judges or lawsuits force their hand.

More than 90 percent of inmates are returned to their communities, so we should do everything we can to ensure that they are ready to return.

We should also ensure that the communities to which they return are ready to receive them. For some time now, Americans have called for harsher prison sentences. In 1994, California voters passed the toughest three-strikes law in the nation, and the state has the largest number of people on death row. However, voters also passed the Substance Abuse and Crime Prevention Act of 2000, which allowed nonviolent drug offenders to go into rehabilitation rather than prison. A study released in 2006 shows that the act reduced incarceration costs substantially (Longshore et al. 2006). As previously mentioned, it seems as if politicians and voters are willing to focus on rehabilitation for nonviolent drug offenders.

As the state of California starts releasing inmates as ordered by *Schwarzenegger v. Plata* (2010) (Richey 2010), residents should take comfort in the fact that these inmates would have been released eventually. Surely, they would not release people on death row, lifers, or high-risk offenders. In fact, the governor could point this out to his fellow Californians. He and other politicians could also point out that sending these men and women home could increase the chance that remaining inmates receive rehabilitation programs that could better prepare them for their eventual release. California officials should also admit that overcrowded prisons do little to help these people become better citizens.

I find it especially interesting that some Californians are upset about the decision to release inmates. If we have faith in our prison systems and believe that they effectively rehabilitate offenders, releasing these inmates early poses few problems. To take this a step farther, if we truly believe that punishment alone reduces crime, then we should really have nothing to worry about. In other words, if rehabilitation programs and college classes reward inmates for bad behavior and all we really need to do is make it tough on them, then what is the problem?

It seems that everyone knows that prisons, especially overcrowded prisons, are not the perfect solution to reducing crime. However, that can change. We can start thinking seriously about changing inmate culture and redirecting their behaviors in more positive ways. We can develop a culture of mutual respect among inmates and prison staff. We can redefine rehabilitation and education programs in prison as rewarding the community and improving public safety. We can give inmates productive things to do with their time. All these things require us to redefine the functions of prison. If we make these efforts, then inmates should have a better shot at actually learning something productive in prison. Otherwise, we force inmates to learn from each other, which may or may not help them once they go on parole.

It is impressive that riots and homicides recently decreased in US prisons (Useem and Piehl 2006). However, more qualitative studies are needed to examine other forms of violence and social control. Future studies should focus on the effectiveness of informal leadership in both men's and women's prisons. Clearly, work is still needed to understand how and why inmates hurt each other.

References

Acker, Joan. 1990. "Hierarchies, Jobs, Bodies: A Theory of Gender Organizations." *Gender and Society* 4:139–158.

Akers, Ronald L., Norman S. Hayner, and Werner Gruninger. 1977. "Prisonization in Five Countries: Type of Prison and Inmate Characteristics." *Criminology* 14:527–554.

Alarid, Leanne Fiftal. 2000. "Sexual Assault and Coercion Among Incarcerated Women Prisoners: Excerpts from Prison Letters." *Prison Journal* 80: 391–406.

Anderson, Elijah. 2000. *Code of the Street: Decency, Violence, and the Moral Life of the Inner City*. New York: W. W. Norton.

Anti-Defamation League. 2005. "Prison Gangs." Washington, DC.

Austin, Paige. 2007. "Inland Prison Remains on Lockdown." [Corona, California] *Press-Enterprise, p.* D2. January 2.

Beck, Allen J., Paige M. Harrison, Marcus Berzofsky, Rachel Caspar, and Christopher Krebs. 2010. "Sexual Victimization in Prisons and Jails Reported by Inmates, 2008–09." Washington, DC: US Department of Justice.

Beck, Allen J., Paige M. Harrison, and Timothy A. Hughes. 2004. "Data Collection for the Prison Rape Elimination Act of 2003." Washington, DC: US Department of Justice, Bureau of Justice Statistics Status Report.

Bedau, Hugo. 1987. *Death Is Different: Studies in the Morality, Law, and Politics of Capital Punishment*. Boston: Northeastern University Press.

Berger, Peter. 1963. *Invitation to Sociology: A Humanistic Perspective*. New York: Doubleday.

Bird, Sharon R. 2003. "De-Gendering Practice/Practicing De-Gendering: Response to Yancy Martin." *Gender and Society* 17:267–369.

Bird, Sharon R., and Leah K. Sokolofski. 2004. "Gendered Socio-Spatial Practices in Public Eating and Drinking Establishments in the United States." *Gender, Place, and Culture* 12:213–230.

Blee, Kathleen M. 2002. *Inside Organized Racism: Women in the Hate Movement*. Berkeley: University of California Press.

Blumer, Herbert. 1969. *Symbolic Interactionism: Perspective and Method.* Berkeley: University of California Press.

Blumstein, Alfred, and Allen J. Beck. 1999. "Population Growth in US Prisons, 1980–1996." Pp. 17–62 in *Prisons*, edited by J. Petersilia and M. Tonry. Chicago: University of Chicago Press.

Bobo, Lawrence, and Camille Zubrinsky. 1996. "Attitudes on Residential Integration: Perceived Status Differences, Mere In-Group Preference, or Racial Prejudice?" *Social Forces* 74:883–909.

Bourdieu, Pierre. 2001. *Masculine Domination.* Palo Alto: Stanford University Press.

Bowker, Lee. 1977. *Prisoner Subcultures.* Lexington: Lexington Press.

Britton, Dana M. 2003. *At Work in the Iron Cage: The Prison as Gendered Organization.* New York: New York University Press.

Burck, Charlotte. 2005. "Comparing Qualitative Research Methodologies for Systemic Research: The Use of Grounded Theory, Discourse Analysis, and Narrative Analysis." *Journal of Family Therapy* 27:237–262.

Bursik, Robert, and Harold Grasmick. 1993. *Neighborhoods and Crime: The Dimensions of Effective Community Control.* Lexington: Lexington Books.

Burton-Rose, Daniel. 2003. "Our Sister's Keepers." Pp. 258–261 in *Prison Nation: The Warehousing of America's Poor*, edited by T. Herivel and P. Wright. New York: Routledge.

Cahill, Spencer. 1989. "Fashioning Males and Females: Appearance Management and Social Reproduction of Gender." *Symbolic Interaction* 12: 281–298.

California Department of Corrections and Rehabilitation. 2003. *California Code of Regulations: Title 15, Crime Prevention and Corrections.* Sacramento.

———. 2006a. "Official Incident Reports." Sacramento.

———. 2006b. "Population (Midyear) Reports." Sacramento.

———. 2007. "Inmate Incidents in Institutions." Sacramento.

———. 2008a. "Census Report." Sacramento.

———. 2008b. "Employees Killed by Inmates." Sacramento.

———. 2009. "Corrections: Moving Forward." Sacramento.

———. 2010. "Institution Statistics." Sacramento.

Charles, Camille. 2000. "Neighborhood Racial-Composition Preferences: Evidence from a Multi-ethnic Metropolis." *Social Problems* 47:379–407.

Charon, Joel. 1998. *Symbolic Interactionism.* Upper Saddle River: Prentice-Hall.

Chesney-Lind, Meda. 2002. "Imprisoning Women: The Unintended Victims of Mass Imprisonment." Pp. 79–94 in *Invisible Punishment: The Collateral Consequences of Mass Imprisonment*, edited by M. Mauer and M. Chesney-Lind. New York: New Press.

Child Welfare League of America. 2003. "Children with Parents in Prison: Child Welfare Policy, Program and Practice Issues." Washington, DC.

Chodorow, Nancy. 1978. *The Reproduction of Mothering.* Berkeley: University of California Press.

Cialdini, Robert B. 1984. *Influence: The Psychology of Persuasion.* New York: HarperCollins Publishers.

Clark, Judith. 1995. "The Impact of the Prison Environment on Mothers." *Prison Journal* 75:306–329.

Clemmer, Donald. 1940. *The Prison Community*. Boston: Christopher Publishing.

Cloward, Richard A. 1960. "Social Control in the Prison." Pp. 20–48 in *Theoretical Studies in Social Organization of the Prison*, edited by R. A. Cloward, D. R. Cressey, G. H. Glosser, R. McCleery, L. E. Ohlin, G. M. Sykes, and S. Messinger. New York: Social Science Research Council.

Connell, R. W. 1987. *Gender and Power: Society, the Person, and Sexual Politics*. Stanford: Stanford University Press.

———. 2000. *The Men and the Boys*. Stanford: Stanford University Press.

Davidenko, Nicolas. 2007. "Silhouetted Face Profiles: A New Methodology for Face Perception Research." *Journal of Vision* 7:1–17.

Davis, Angela. 2006. "Race and Criminalization: Black Americans and the Punishment Industry." Pp. 244–254 in *Rethinking the Color Line: Readings in Race and Ethnicity*, edited by C. A. Gallagher. New York: McGraw-Hill.

Denzin, Norman, and Yvonna Lincoln. 1998. "Entering the Field of Qualitative Research." Pp. 1–34 in *Strategies of Qualitative Inquiry*, edited by N. Denzin and Y. Lincoln. Beverly Hills: Sage.

Donaldson, Stephen. 2001. "A Million Jockers, Punks, and Queens." Pp. 118–126 in *Prison Masculinities*, edited by D. Sabo, T. A. Kupers, and W. London. Philadelphia: Temple University Press.

———. 2003. "Hooking Up: Protective Pairing for Punks." Pp. 348–353 in *Violence in War and Peace: An Anthology*, edited by N. Scheper-Hughes and P. Bourgois. Williston: Blackwell.

Duneier, Mitchell. 2001. "On the Evolution of Sidewalk." Pp. 167–187 in *Contemporary Field Research: Perspectives and Formulations*, edited by R. M. Emerson. Prospect Heights: Waveland Press.

Eder, Donna, Catherine Evans, and Stephen Parker. 1997. *School Talk: Gender and Adolescent Culture*. New Brunswick: Rutgers University.

Eschholz, Sarah, and Jana Bufkin. 2001. "Crime in the Movies: Investigating the Efficacy of Measures of Both Sex and Gender for Predicting Victimization and Offending in Film." *Sociological Forum* 16:655–676.

Federal Bureau of Investigation. 2007. "Index of Violent Crime." Washington, DC.

Fields, Gary. 2009. "White House Czar Calls for End to 'War on Drugs.'" *Wall Street Journal*, p. A3. May 4.

Fine, Gary Alan. 1984. "Negotiated Orders and Organizational Cultures." *Annual Review of Sociology* 10:239–262.

Fischer, Ryan. 2005. "Are California's Recidivism Rates Really the Highest in the Nation? It Depends on What Measure of Recidivism You Use." Irvine: Center for Evidence-Based Corrections.

Fleisher, Mark, and Jessie Krienert. 2009. *The Myth of Prison Rape: Sexual Culture in American Prisons*. Lanham: Rowman and Littlefield

Forsyth, Craig J., Rhonda D. Evans, and D. Burk Foster. 2002. "An Analysis of Inmate Explanations for Lesbian Relationships in Prison." *International Journal of Sociology of the Family* 30:66–77.

Foster, Theresa. 1975. "Make-Believe Families: A Response of Women and Girls to the Deprivations of Imprisonment." *International Journal of Criminology and Penology* 3:71–78.

Fox, James A., and Marianne Zawitz. 2004. "Homicide Trends in the United States: 2002 Update." Washington, DC: US Department of Justice.

Gaes, Gerald G., and Andrew L. Goldberg. 2004. "Prison Rape: A Critical Review of the Literature." Washington, DC: National Institute of Justice.

Giallombardo, Rose. 1974. *The Social World of Imprisoned Girls*. New York: John Wiley Publishing.

Gibbons, John J., and Nicholas de B. Katzenbach. 2006. *Confronting Confinement: A Report of the Commission on Safety and Abuse in America's Prisons*. Washington, DC: Commission on Safety and Abuse in America's Prisons.

Gillespie, L. Kay. 2000. *Dancehall Ladies*. New York: University Press of America.

Gilligan, Carol. 1982. *In a Different Voice*. Boston: Harvard University Press.

Girshick, Lori B. 2000. *No Safe Haven: Stories of Women in Prison*. Boston: Northeastern University Press.

Glaze, Lauren E. 2010. "Correctional Populations in the United States, 2009." Washington, DC: US Department of Justice, Bureau of Justice Statistics.

Goffman, Erving. 1959. *The Presentation of Self in Everyday Life*. New York: Doubleday.

———. 1961. *Asylums: Essays on the Social Situation of Mental Patients and Other Inmates*. New York: Doubleday.

———. 1983. "The Interaction Order: American Sociological Association, 1982 Presidential Address." *American Sociological Review* 48:1–17.

Goldstone, Jack A., and Bert Useem. 1999. "Prison Riots as Microrevolutions: An Extension of State-Centered Theories." *American Journal of Sociology* 104:985–1029.

Goodey, Jo. 1995. "Fear of Crime: Children and Gendered Socialization." Pp. 295–312 in *Gender and Crime*, edited by R. E. Dobash, R. P. Dobash, and L. Noaks. Cardiff: University of Wales Press.

Goodman, Philip. 2008. "It's Just Black, White, or Hispanic: An Observational Study of Racializing Moves in California's Segregated Prison Reception Center." *Law and Society Review* 42:735–770.

Gornick, Janet C., and David S. Meyer. 1998. "Changing Political Opportunity: The Anti-Rape Movement and Public Policy." *Journal of Policy History* 10:366–398.

Greenfeld, Lawrence A., and Tracy L. Snell. 1999. "Women Offenders." Washington, DC: US Department of Justice, Bureau of Justice Statistics.

Greer, Kimberly R. 2000. "The Changing Nature of Interpersonal Relationships in a Women's Prison." *Prison Journal* 80:442–468.

Hagen, John, Hans Merkens, and Klaus Boehnke. 1995. "Delinquency and Disdain: Social Capital and the Control of Right-Wing Extremism Among East and West Berlin Youth." *American Journal of Sociology* 100:1028–1052.

Hampton, Blanche. 1993. *Prisons and Women*. Kensington: New South Wales University Press.

Harer, Miles D., and Neal P. Langan. 2001. "Gender Differences in Predictors of Prison Violence: Assessing the Predictive Validity of a Risk Classification System." *Crime and Delinquency* 47:513–536.

Harrison, Paige M., and Allen J. Beck. 2006. "Prisoners in 2005." Washington, DC: US Department of Justice, Office of Justice Programs.

Hassine, Victor. 2007. *Life Without Parole: Living in Prison Today*. Edited by R. Johnson and A. Dobrzanska. Oxford: Oxford University Press.

Hayner, Norman S., and Ellis Ash. 1940. "The Prison as a Community." *American Sociological Review* 5:577–583.

Henderson, Martha L., Francis T. Cullen, and Leo Carrol. 2000. "Race, Rights, and Order in Prisons: A National Survey of Wardens on the Radical Integration of Prison Cells." *Prison Journal* 80:295–308.

Hirschi, Travis. 1969. *Causes of Delinquency*. Chicago: University of Chicago Press.

Hollander, Jocelyn A. 2001. "Vulnerability and Dangerousness: The Construction of Gender Through Conversation About Violence." *Gender and Society* 15:83–109.

Human Rights Watch. 2001. "World Report 2001: United States." New York.

Human Rights Watch Women's Rights Project. 1996. "All Too Familiar: Sexual Abuse of Women in US State Prisons." New York.

Humes, Karen R., Nicholas Jones, and Roberto Ramirez. 2011. "Overview of Race and Hispanic Origin." Washington, DC: US Bureau of the Census.

Hunt, Geoffrey, Stephanie Reigel, Thomas Morales, and Dan Waldorf. 1993. "Changes in Prison Culture: Prison Gangs and the Case of the 'Pepsi Generation.'" *Social Problems* 40:398–409.

Iadicola, Peter, and Anson Shupe. 2003. *Violence, Inequality, and Human Freedom*. New York: Rowman and Littlefield.

Irwin, John. 1970. *The Felon*. Englewood Cliffs: Prentice-Hall.

———. 1980. *Prisons in Turmoil*. Boston: Little, Brown.

Irwin, John, and Donald R. Cressey. 1962. "Thieves, Convicts, and the Inmate Culture." *Social Problems* 10:142–155.

Jacobs, James B. 1977. *Stateville: The Penitentiary in Mass Society*. Chicago: University of Chicago Press.

Jenness, Valerie, Cheryl L. Maxson, Kristy N. Matsuda, and Jennifer M. Sumner. 2007. "Violence in California Correctional Facilities: An Empirical Examination of Sexual Assault." Report to the California Department of Corrections and Rehabilitation. Sacramento.

Kornhauser, Ruth R. 1978. *Social Causes of Delinquency*. Chicago: University of Chicago Press.

Krivo, Lauren, Ruth Peterson, and Danielle Kuhl. 2009. "Segregation, Racial Structure, and Neighborhood Violent Crime." *American Journal of Sociology* 114:1765–1802.

Kupers, Terry A. 2001. "Rape and the Prison Code." Pp. 111–126 in *Prison Masculinities*, edited by D. Sabo, T. A. Kupers, and W. London. Philadelphia: Temple University Press.

Leger, Robert. 1987. "Lesbianism Among Women Prisoners: Participants and Nonparticipants." *Criminal Justice Behavior* 14:463–479.

Liptak, Adam. 2008. "1 in 100 US Adults Behind Bars, New Study Says." *New York Times*, p. B1. February 28.

Longshore, Douglas, Angela Hawken, Darren Urada, and M. Douglas Anglin. 2006. "Evaluation of the Substance Abuse and Crime Prevention Act." Integrated Substance Abuse Programs, University of California, Los Angeles.

MacKenzie, Doris L., James W. Robinson, and Carol S. Campbell. 1989. "Long-Term Incarceration of Female Offenders." *Criminal Justice and Behavior* 16:223–238.

Maines, David. 1982. "In Search of Mesostructure: Studies in the Negotiated Order." *Urban Life* 11:267–279.

Maines, David, and Joy Charlton. 1985. "Negotiated Order Approach to the Analysis of Social Organization." *Studies in Social Interaction* 1: 271–308.

Martin, Patricia Yancy. 2003. "Saying and Doing Vs. Said and Done: Gendering Practices, Practicing Gender at Work." *Gender and Society* 17: 342–366.

———. 2004. "Gender as a Social Institution." *Social Forces* 82:1249–1273.

Massey, Douglas S., and Nancy A. Denton. 1993. *American Apartheid: Segregation and the Making of the Underclass*. Cambridge: Harvard University Press.

Mauer, Marc, and Meda Chesney-Lind. 2002. *Invisible Punishment: The Collateral Consequences of Mass Imprisonment*. New York: New York Press.

McGuffey, Shawn, and Lindsey Rich. 1999. "Playing in the Gender Transgression Zone: Race, Class, and Hegemonic Masculinity in Middle Childhood." *Gender and Society* 13:608–630.

Meachum, Larry. 2000. "Prisons: Breeding Grounds for Hate?" *Corrections Today* 62:130–133.

Messerschmidt, James W. 2006. "Masculinities and Crime: Beyond a Dualist Criminology." Pp. 29–43 in *Rethinking Gender, Crime, and Justice*, edited by C. M. Renzetti, L. Goodstein, and S. L. Miller. Los Angeles: Roxbury.

Miller, Jody. 2001. *One of the Guys: Gangs and Gender*. New York: Oxford University Press.

Moore, Joan W. 1991. *Going Down to the Barrio: Homeboys and Homegirls in Change*. Philadelphia: Temple University Press.

Nathan, Maria, and Ian Mitroff. 1991. "The Use of Negotiated Order Theory as a Tool for the Analysis and Development of an Interorganizational Field." *Journal of Applied Behavioral Science* 27:163–180.

Orlando-Morningstar, Denise. 1997. "Prison Gangs." Report for the Federal Judicial Center: Special Needs Offenders Bulletin. Washington, DC.

O'Sullivan, Sean. 2006. "Representations of Prison in Nineties Hollywood Cinema: From *Con Air* to the *Shawshank Redemption*." Pp. 483–498 in *Behind Bars: Readings on Prison Culture*, edited by R. Tewksbury. Upper Saddle River: Pearson.

Owen, Barbara. 1998. *In the Mix: Struggle and Survival in a Woman's Prison*. New York: State University of Albany Press.

Parenti, Christian. 1999. *Lockdown America: Police and Prisons in the Age of Crisis*. London: Verso.

Parker, Karen F., Mari A. Dewees, and Michael L. Radelet. 2001. "Racial Bias and the Conviction of the Innocent." Pp. 114–134 in *Wrongly Convicted: Perspectives on Failed Justice*, edited by S. D. Westervelt and J. A. Humphrey. New Brunswick: Rutgers University Press.

Perry, Tony. 2006. "US Indicts 36 in Mexican Mafia Crackdown." *Los Angeles Times*. June 17.

Petersilia, Joan. 2003. *When Prisoners Come Home: Parole and Prisoner Reentry*. New York: Oxford University Press.

Pinar, William, F. 2001. *The Gender of Racial Politics and Violence in America: Lynching, Prison Rape, and the Crisis of Masculinity*. New York: Peter Lang.

Pollack, William. 1999. *Real Boys: Rescuing Our Sons from the Myth of Boyhood*. New York: Henry Holt.

Pollock, Joycelyn M. 1997. *Prison: Today and Tomorrow*. Gaithersburg: Aspen Press.

———. 1998. *Counseling Women in Prison*. Thousand Oaks: Sage.

Pollock, Joycelyn M., and Sareta M. Davis. 2005. "The Continuing Myth of the Violent Female Offender." *Criminal Justice Review* 30:5–29.

Polsky, Ned. 2006. *Hustlers, Beats, and Others*. Piscataway: Aldine Transaction.

Propper, Alice M. 1982. "Make-Believe Families and Homosexuality Among Imprisoned Girls." *Criminology* 20:127–139.

Reiman, Jeffrey. 2001. *The Rich Get Richer and the Poor Get Prison: Ideology, Class, and Criminal Justice*. Boston: Allyn and Bacon.

Reissman, Catherine. 1993. *Narrative Analysis*. Newbury Park: Sage.

Renzetti, Claire M. 2006. "Gender and Violent Crime." Pp. 93–107 in *Rethinking Gender, Crime, and Justice*, edited by C. M. Renzetti, L. Goodstein, and S. L. Miller. Los Angeles: Roxbury.

Richey, Warren. 2010. "Supreme Court to Hear California Prison Overcrowding Case." *Christian Science Monitor*. June 14.

Risling, Greg. 2006. "Prosecutors Ready Closing Arguments in Aryan Brotherhood Case." Associated Press. July 11.

Sampson, Robert J., and Lydia Bean. 2006. "Cultural Mechanisms and Killing Fields." Pp. 8–36 in *The Many Colors of Crime*, edited by R. Peterson, L. Krivo, and J. Hagan. New York: New York University Press.

Sampson, Robert J., and John H. Laub. 1994. "Urban Poverty and the Family Context of Delinquency." *Child Development* 65:523–540.

Schrag, Clarence. 1954. "Leadership Among Prison Inmates." *American Sociological Review* 19:37–42.

Schwarzenegger, Arnold. 2010. "The Signing of Senate Bill 1449." *Letter to California Senate*. http://www.salem-news.com/articles/october012010/schwarzenegger-marijuana.php

Scott, Susie. 2009. "Re-Clothing the Emperor: The Swimming Pool as a Negotiated Order." *Symbolic Interaction* 32:123–145.

Simi, Pete. 2010. *American Swastika: Inside the White Power Movement's Hidden Spaces of Hate*. Lanham: Rowman and Littlefield.

Smith, Brenda V. 1998. "An End to Silence: Women Prisoner's Handbook on Identifying and Addressing Sexual Misconduct." Washington, DC: National Women's Law Center.

Snow, David A., and Leon Anderson. 1993. *Down on Their Luck: A Study of Homeless Street People*. Berkeley: University of California Press.

Soto, Onell. 2006. "36 Indicted in Mexican Mafia Crackdown." *San Diego Union Tribune*. June 17.

Southern Poverty Law Center. 2001. "Active US Hate Groups in 2001." Montgomery.

Stanko, Elizabeth. 2001. "Women, Danger, and Criminology." Pp. 11–22 in *Women, Crime, and Criminal Justice*, edited by C. M. Renzetti and L. Goodstein. Los Angeles: Roxbury.

Sterling, Eric E. 1998. "Racially Disproportionate Outcomes in Processing Drug Cases." Washington, DC: Criminal Justice Policy Foundation.

Stowell, Jacob, and James Byrne. 2008. "Does What Happens in Prison Stay in Prison? Examining the Reciprocal Relationship Between Community and Prison Culture." Pp. 27–39 in *The Culture of Prison Violence*, edited by J. Byrne, D. Hummer, and F. Taxman. Boston: Pearson.

Struckman-Johnson, Cindy, David Struckman-Johnson, Lila Rucker, Kurt Bumby, and Stephen Donaldson. 1996. "Sexual Coercion Reported by Men and Women in Prison." *Journal of Sex Research* 33:67–76.

Sumner, Jennifer M., and Kristy N. Matsuda. 2006. "Shining Light in Dark Corners: An Overview of Prison Rape Elimination Legislation and Introduction to Current Research." Irvine: Center for Evidence-Based Corrections.

Swidler, Ann. 1986. "Culture in Action: Symbols and Strategies." *American Sociological Review* 51:273–286.

Sykes, Gresham M. 1958. *The Society of Captives: A Study of a Maximum Security Prison*. Princeton: Princeton University Press.

Tajfel, Henri, and John Turner. 1979. "An Integrative Theory of Intergroup Conflict." Pp. 33–47 in *The Social Psychology of Intergroup Relations*, edited by W. Austin and S. Worchel. Monterey: Brooks/Cole.

Talvi, Silja J. A. 2003. "Not Part of My Sentence." Pp. 262–268 in *Prison Nation: The Warehousing of America's Poor*, edited by T. Herivel and P. Wright. New York: Routledge.

Taylor, Ralph B. 1996. "Neighborhood Responses to Disorder and Local Attachments: The Systemic Model of Attachment, Social Disorganization, and Neighborhood Use Value." *Sociological Forum* 11:41–74.

———. 1997. "Social Order and Disorder of Street Blocks and Neighborhoods: Ecology, Microecology, and the Systemic Model of Social Disorganization." *Journal of Research in Crime and Delinquency* 34:34–65.

Terry, Charles. 1997. "The Function of Humor for Prison Inmates." *Journal of Contemporary Criminal Justice* 13:23–40.

Thorne, Barrie. 1993. *Gender Play: Girls and Boys in School*. New Brunswick: Rutgers University Press.

———. 1998. "Girls and Boys Together . . . But Mostly Apart: Gender Arrangements in Elementary School." Pp. 81–100 in *Men's Lives*, edited by M. Kimmel and M. Messner. Boston: Allyn and Bacon.

Tittle, Charles R. 1995. *Control Balance: Toward a General Theory of Deviance*. Boulder: Westview Press.

Tittle, Charles R., and Drollene P. Tittle. 1964. "Social Organization of Prisoners: An Empirical Test." *Social Forces* 43:216–221.

Toch, Hans. 2002. *Acting Out: Maladaptive Behavior in Confinement*. Washington, DC: American Psychological Association.

Toch, Hans, and Kenneth Adams. 1989. *Coping: Maladaption in Prison*. New Brunswick: Transaction Press.

Tonry, Michael. 1995. *Malign Neglect: Race, Crime, and Punishment in America*. New York: Oxford University Press.

————. 1999. "Sentencing and Corrections: Issues for the 21st Century." Washington, DC: US Department of Justice.

Tonry, Michael, and Richard Frase. 2001. *Sentencing and Sanctions in Western Countries*. Oxford: Oxford University Press.

Trammell, Rebecca. 2009a. "Relational Violence in Women's Prison: How Women Describe Interpersonal Violence and Gender." *Women and Criminal Justice* 19:267–285.

————. 2009b. "Values, Rules, and Keeping the Peace: How Men Describe Order and the Inmate Code in California Prisons." *Deviant Behavior: An Interdisciplinary Journal* 32:334–350.

Trammell, Rebecca, and Scott Chenault. 2009. "We Have to Take These Guys Out: Motivations for Assaulting Incarcerated Child Molesters." *Symbolic Interaction* 32:334–350.

Trulson, Chad R., and James W. Marquart. 2009. *First Available Cell: Desegregation of the Texas Prison System*. Austin: University of Texas Press.

US Department of Justice, Bureau of Justice Statistics. 2005. "Nation's Prison and Jail Population Grew by 932 Inmates per Week: Number of Female Inmates Reached More Than 100,000." Washington DC.

Useem, Bert. 1985. "Disorganization and the New Mexico Prison Riot of 1980." *American Sociological Review* 50:677–688.

Useem, Bert, Camille Graham Camp, and George M. Camp. 1996. *Resolution of Prison Riots: Strategies and Policies*. New York: Oxford University Press.

Useem, Bert, and Peter A. Kimball. 1987. "A Theory of Prison Riots." *Theory and Society* 15:87–122.

————. 1991. *States of Siege: US Prison Riots 1971–1986*. New York: Oxford University Press.

Useem, Bert, and Anne M. Piehl. 2006. "Prison Buildup and Disorder." *Punishment and Society* 8:87–115.

Vaghan, Graham, Henri Tajfel, and Jennifer Williams. 1981. "Bias in Reward Allocation in an Intergroup Interpersonal Context." *Social Psychology Quarterly* 44:37–42.

Valentine, Gill. 1992. "Images of Danger: Women's Sources of Information About Spatial Distribution of Male Violence." *Area* 24:22–29.

Vryan, Kevin D., Patricia A. Adler, and Peter Adler. 2003. "Identity." Pp. 367–390 in *Handbook of Symbolic Interaction*, edited by L. T. Reynolds. Lanham: AltaMira Press.

Wacquant, Loïc. 2001. "Deadly Symbiosis: When Ghetto and Prison Meet and Mesh." Pp. 82–120 in *Mass Imprisonment: Social Causes and Consequences*, edited by D. Garland. London: Sage.

Warren, Jenifer. 2004. "Prison Held Gang Members in Lockdown for Almost 2 Years." *Los Angeles Times*. April 8.

Wilkinson, Reginald A., and Tessa Unwin. 1999. "Intolerance in Prison: A Recipe for Disaster." *Corrections Today* 61:98.

Winfree, Tom, Greg Newbold, and Huston Tubb. 2002. "Prisoner Perspectives on Inmate Culture in New Mexico and New Zealand." *Prison Journal* 82:213–233.

Zimbardo, Philip. 2008. *The Lucifer Effect: Understanding How Good People Turn Evil*. New York: Random House.

Zimbardo, Philip, Craig Haney, Curtis Banks, and D. Jaffe. 1974. "The Psychology of Imprisonment: Privation Power and Pathology." Pp. 61–73 in *Doing Unto Others: Explorations in Social Behavior*, edited by Z. Rubin. Englewood Cliffs: Prentice-Hall.

Index

About the Book

Is it possible that a prison's gangs, racial tensions, and underground economy may actually serve to make it a less dangerous place? In this examination of violence behind bars, Rebecca Trammell illuminates the social code that prisoners enforce—in defiance of official rules and regulations—to maintain a predictable order.

Trammell also compares the experiences of male and female prisoners, underscoring the role of gender and sexual assault in shaping life behind bars. Equally important, she explores the significance of prison culture for the fate of convicts when they leave the prison environment.

Rebecca Trammell is assistant professor of criminology and criminal justice at the University of Nebraska at Omaha.